Mac 365

. . . .

Kenneth Cardell

Produced by:

FriesenPress
Suite 300 – 852 Fort Street
Victoria, BC, Canada V8W 1H8

www.friesenpress.com

Distributed to the trade by The Ingram Book Company

A special thank you and a massive macaroni HUG to Emma Lotto and Adeline Niccoli for your dedicated and heartfelt work on this book. Mac 365 has been in the oven for years, and with your unique touch and fabulous style, it's now ready to serve. This book could not have been completed without you - who needs flowers when I have you two!

Table of Contents

Attention People, Mr. Mac Everyday!   1

The Kenneth Cardell Story   2

Mac, Going Way Back   4

Using Mac-365   5

Recipe Reference   295

Uses for Cheese Powder   297

Closing Remarks   299

Recipes: Mac-365

What's in the Fridge? Mac & Cheese

Appetizers & Soups
(pages 7 – 17)

Crab Mac & Cheese Mushroom Caps

Macastrone Soup

Mac & Cheese Bruschetta

Mac & Cheese with Pico de Gallo

Pesto Mac & Feta Portobello Caps

Mac & Cheese Poppers

Na'Cho Average Mac & Cheese

Mac-erranean Dip

Angels on Horseback Mac and Cheese

Addie's Nibbles

Mac & Cheese French Onion Soup

Mac & Cheese Seven Layer Dip

Cheddar Cheese Soup

Mac 'n' Eggs
(pages 18 – 25)

Mac & Cheese Meat Lover's Eggs Strata

Blue Plate Special Mac & Cheese

Mac & Cheese Waffles

Quiche a là Mac et Fromage

Bacon and Eggs Mac & Cheese

Mac & Cheese French Toast

BMB Mac & Cheese Quiche

Mac & Cheese Bacon Broccoli Frittata

Mile High City Mac & Cheese

Mac 'n' Greens
(pages 26 – 38)

Antipasto Mac & Cheese Salad

Mac & Cheese Chicken Salad

MacaRoma Salad

Mac & Cheese Salad Nicoise

Mac & Cheese Pasta Salad with Salami

Mac & Cheese Rainbow Salad

Mac & Cheese Waldorf Salad

Smoked Salmon Mac & Cheese Salad

Mac & Cheese Coleslaw

Cobb Mac & Cheese Salad

Deli Mac & Cheese Salad

Spring Fling Mac & Cheese Salad

Mac & Cheese Three Bean Salad

Mac & Cheese Peach Salad

Mac & Cheese Caesar Salad

Mac Du Canada
(pages 39 – 46)

Canuck Mac & Cheese

Wet Coast Mac & Cheese

Mon Dieu Mac & Cheese

Home on the Range Mac & Cheese

Wheat -Treat Mac & Cheese

Golden Boy Mac & Cheese

Drive By the Lake Mac & Cheese

Ocean of Love Mac & Cheese

Wicked Mac & Cheese

Kiss the Cod Mac & Cheese

Dive for a Pearl Mac & Cheese

The Wreck of Yellowknife Mac & Cheese

Dawson City Sour Toe Mac & Cheese

On Ice Mac & Cheese

United States of Mac & Cheese
(pages 47 – 76)

Alabama Slammer Mac & Cheese

Juno Salmon Mac & Cheese

Chili Mac & Cheese

Spiked Mac & Cheese

Armadilla Thrilla Mac & Cheese

Health Club Mac & Cheese

Sunny Side Up Mac & Cheese

Chuck Mac & Cheese

State Pride Mac & Cheese

Plantation Nation Mac & Cheese

Conked Out Mac & Cheese

Fly the Coup Mac & Cheese

Hang Ten Mac & Cheese

Potatoes Mac & Cheese Surprise

"Cheese Head" Mac & Cheese

Train Wreck Mac & Cheese

Gary Wants You Mac & Cheese

Des Moines Mac & Cheese Salad

Wild West BBQ Mac & Cheese

Trouble Chicken Mac & Cheese

Ragin' Cajun Mac & Cheese

Lux Lobster Mac & Cheese

Blue Crab Delight

Upside Down Mac & Cheese

Takin' a Lickin' Mac & Cheese

With the Soda Mac & Cheese

Mudflats Mac & Cheese

St. Louis Blues Mac & Cheese

Wagon Wheel Special Mac & Cheese

Flap in the Wind Mac & Cheese

Jumpin' Beans Mac & Cheese

All-In Lucky Duck Mac & Cheese

Live Free or Die Mac & Cheese

Turn Pike Mac & Cheese

Dog City Mac & Cheese

By the Sea Mac & Cheese

Pleasant Pheasant Mac & Cheese

Bam Bam Mac & Cheese

Ocean Spin Mac & Cheese

Philly Mac & Cheese

Road Kill Mac & Cheese

Dilly Shrimp Mac & Cheese

Hop 'n' Go Mac & Cheese

Slap Happy Mac & Cheese

Roll Over Mac & Cheese

Alamo Mac & Cheese

Ella Bella Mac & Cheese

Sweetheart Chicken Mac & Cheese

Silent Sam Mac & Cheese

Pacific Coast Highway Mac & Cheese

Country Roads Mac & Cheese

Where the Buffalo Roam Mac & Cheese

Macronesia Mac & Cheese

Curry in a Hurry Mac & Cheese

Phantom Mac & Cheese

Passion Mac & Cheese

On a Roll Mac & Cheese

Mac & Cheese in the Jolly Ole United Kingdom
(pages 77 – 80)

Mac & Cheese Shepherds Pie

Luke's Bangers & Mac

Bubbles and Squeak Mac & Cheese

Rolling Hills Mac & Cheese

Stone Cottage Mac & Cheese

Mamma Mia Mac & Cheese
(pages 81 – 96)

Mac & Cheese Skillet Cacciatore

MacAmore

Italian Chorizo Mac & Cheese Pie

Mac & Cheese Bolognese

Mac & Cheese Lasagna

Chicken Parmesan Mac & Cheese

On Top of Old Macky

Mac & Cheese Primavera

Baked Caprese Mac & Cheese

Pancetta Mac & Fromaggio

Mac & Cheese alla Carbonara

Chicken Marbella Mac & Cheese

Tetrazzini Mac & Cheese

Chicken Piccata Mac & Cheese

Mac & Cheese Bologna Bowls

Mac & Cheese Chorizo Lasagna

Mac & Cheese Florentine

Mac & Cheese Takes Europe
(pages 97 – 118)

Coq au Vin Mac & Cheese

Savory Mac & Cheese Crepes

Spanish Mac & Cheese Casserole

Mac & Blue Cheese Bomb

Mac & Cheese Seafood Pancetta Paella

Shainey's Mac & Cheese Cordon Bleu

Danny's Baked Mac & Cheese Pie

Creamy Chicken Mac & Cheese Bake

Mac & Cheese Chicken Casserole

Margaret's Chicken Broccoli Mac & Cheese

There is a Heaven Mac & Cheese

I'll Be Bock Mac & Cheese

Mac & Cheese with Anchovies and Garlic

Mac & Cheese with Clam Sauce

Mac & Cheese with Ham and Spinach

Mac & Cheese Stuffed Potatoes

Mac & Cheese Chorizo Bean Cassoulet

Bacon Gruyere Onion Mac & Cheese

Matterhorn Mac & Cheese

Mac & Cheese Pepper Chicken Skillet

Savory Mac & Cream Cheese Pie

Mac & Cheese Thyme Chicken Bake

Mac & Cheese Stuffed Bell Peppers

Roasted Chicken with Mac & Cheese

Mac & Cheese with Peas and Bacon

Mac & Cheese with Scallops

Mac & Cheese Visits Eastern Europe
(pages 119 – 125)

Mac & Cheese Chicken Kiev

Mac & Cheese Rueben

Mac & Cheese with Ukrainian Sausage

Mac & Cheese Cabbage Rolls

Gouda Spinach Salami Mac & Cheese

Cabbage and Prosciutto Mac & Cheese

Mac & Cheese Kielbasa and Sauerkraut

Mac & Cheese Beef Stroganoff

Mac & Cheese Perogies

Mac-erranean
(pages 126 – 142)

Classic Moussaka Mac & Cheese

Sicilian Mac & Cheese Pizza

Chicken Souvlaki Mac & Cheese

Spanakopita Mac & Cheese Muffins

My Big Fat Toga Mac & Cheese

Mac & Cheese Tabouli

Mac & Cheese Falafel

Marrakesh Mac & Cheese

Mac & Cheese Lemon Herb Chicken

Chicken and Artichoke Mac & Cheese

Mac & Cheese Pastitsio

Greek Mac & Cheese Dinner

Hummus and Pita Mac & Cheese

Mediterranean Mac & Cheese

Chickpea and Parsley Mac & Cheese

Tzatziki Mac & Cheese Salad

Artichoke Olive Mac & Feta Cheese

Mac & Cheese with Lentils

Sun-dried Tomato Chicken Mac & Cheese

East Meets West Mac & Cheese
(pages 143 – 160)

Pad Thai Mac & Cheese

Mac & Cheese Sushi

Chopsticks Mac & Cheese

Mac & Cheese Steak Stir-Fry

Kung Pao Chicken Mac & Cheese

Thai One on Mac & Cheese

Oyakodon Mac & Cheese

Miso Lucky Mac & Cheese

Thai Peanut Chicken Mac & Cheese

Sweet and Sour Chicken Mac & Cheese

Mac & Cheese with Wicked Asian Greens

Spicy Chicken Stir-Fry Mac & Cheese

Sesame Beef Broccoli Mac & Cheese

Szechuan Chicken Mac & Cheese

Forbidden City Mac & Cheese

Cran Orange Chicken Mac & Cheese

Mac & Cheese Rice Bowl

Mac & Cheese Nasi Goreng

Mac & Cheese California Roll

Mumbai Okra Mac & Cheese

Madras Mac & Cheese

Oriental Mac & Cheese with Tuna

Mac & Cheese Heads South
(pages 161 – 166)

Mac & Cheese Jambalaya

Bayou Shrimp Po' Boy Mac & Cheese

Crab Creamed Spinach Mac & Cheese

Honey Pecan Chicken Mac & Cheese

Hey Macarena Mac & Cheese

New Orleans Blues Mac & Cheese

Mac & Cheese with Andouille Sausage

Fried Green Tomatoes Mac & Cheese

Frontier Mac & Cheese
(pages 167 – 193)

Blazin' Saddles Mac & Cheese

Burrito Pie in the Sky Mac & Cheese

Fiesta Mac & Cheese Bake

Mac & Cheese Quesadillas

Mac & Cheese Taco Salad Olé!

Mexican Chorizo Mac & Cheese

Sombrero Mac & Cheese

Mexico City Mac & Cheese Lasagna

Taos Chicken Mac & Cheese

Tex-Mex Mac & Cheese

Hoedown Mac & Cheese

Mac & Cheese Baja Taco

Chipotle and Onion Mac & Cheese

Corn and Green Chile Mac & Cheese

Campfire Mac & Cheese

Buffalo Chicken Mac & Cheese

Chiapas Mac & Cheese

Mac & Cheese Double B Enchiladas

Mac & Cheese Fiesta Tacos

Hatch Chile Mac & Cheese

Salsa Verde Chicken Mac & Cheese

Ride 'Em Cowboy Mac & Cheese Stew

South of the Border Mac & Cheese

Texas Caviar Mac & Cheese

Tijuana Mac & Cheese Enchiladas

Sufferin' Succotash Mac & Cheese

Oaxaca Mac & Cheese

Mac & Cheese Black Bean Burritos

Bandana Mac & Cheese

Mac & Cheese Goes For A Dip
(pages 194 – 206)

Mac & Cheese Crab Cakes

Amalfi Coast Halibut Mac & Cheese

NYC Style Mac & Cheese

Crabby Mac & Cheese

Goddess Mac & Cheese

Lobster Mac & Cheese

Mac & Cheese Shrimp Primavera

"Go To" Mac & Cheese

Salmon Dill Mac & Cream Cheese

Herby Shrimp Mac & Cheese

Luxury Fish Pie Mac & Cheese

Mac & Cheese with Mussels

Ladies Who Lunch Mac & Cheese

Super Luxe Seafood Mac & Cheese

Shrimp Scampi Mac & Cheese

Mac & Cheese Takes Veggies for a Spin
(pages 207 – 244)

Alex's Vegan Mac & Cheese

Balsamic Pumpkin Mac & Cheese

Cheesy Crusty Crunch Mac & Cheese

Crème Fraiche Mac & Cheese

Crunchy Munchy Mac & Cheese

Don't Be a Square Mac & Cheese

Dynamite Mac & Cheese

Bring the Bling Mac & Cheese

Garlicky Tomato Mac & Cheese

Casetta Mac & Cheese

Parsley Pesto Mac & Three Cheese Bake

Harvest Time Mac & Cheese

Italian Stallion Mac & Cheese

Cherry Pepper Mac & Cheese

Woodland Mac & Cheese

S'More Mac & Cheese

Au Gratin Mac & Cheese

Hearty Mac & Cheese

Mac & Trio Cheese Minis

Herby Mushroom Mac & Cheese

Hippy Dippy Mac & Cheese

Garden Variety Mac & Cheese

Brocco-flower Mac & Cheese

Cheezy Tomato Mac & Cheese

Double "S" Mac & Cheese

Deep Fried Mac & Cheese

Mac & Leek

Ring the Bell Mac & Cheese

Zany Zucchini Mac & Cheese

Luv Boat Mac & Cheese

Power-up Mac & Cheese

Magic Mushroom Mac & Cheese

Mint Cilantro Mac & Cheese

Health Nut Mac & Cheese

Puttin' On the Ritz Mac & Cheese Pie

Mac & Cheese Arrosto

Triple Threat Mac & Cheese

Classic Combo Mac & Cheese

Sunny Outlook Mac & Cheese

OMG Pear Rosemary Mac & Gorgonzola

Vitamin C Booster Mac & Cheese

Mac & Cheese Gets Dressed Up
(pages 245 – 251)

Thanksgiving Mac & Cheese

O Canada Mac & Cheese

Happy New Year Mac & Cheese

Red White and Bleu Mac & Cheese

Valentine's Day Mac & Cheese

Jack O' Lantern Mac & Cheese

St. Patrick's Day Mac & Cheese

Seasons Greetings Mac & Cheese

Easter Mac & Cheese

Smacwiches
(pages 252 - 264)

Mac & Cheese Clubhouse

Meatloaf Mac & Cheese Smacwich

Philly Mac & Cheese Steak Wonder

California Dreamin' Mac & Cheese

Bacon Avocado and PB Mac & Cheese

Posh Mac & Cheese Smacwich

Mac & Cheese Meatball Subs

ABC's Grilled Mac & Cheese Smacwich

Grilled Mac & Cheese Smacwich

BBQ Mac & Cheese Burgers

Mac & Cheese Joes

Croque Monsieur Mac & Cheese

Mac & Cheese with Turkey and Cheddar

Rock Star Mac & Cheese Smacwich

Monte Cristo Mac & Cheese

Croque Señor Mac & Cheese Havana

Elvis Has Left the Building Mac & Cheese

Grilled Jalapeño Mac & Cream Cheese

5 Star Style Mac & Cheese
(pages 265 - 280)

We Be Jammin' Mac & Cheese

Herby Squash Mac & Cheese

Mike, Mac and Tenderloins

Jersey Shore Mac & Cheese

Surf and Turf Mac & Cheese Bake

Mac & Cheese Deluxe Hawaiian Pizza

In-Laws Dinner Mac & Cheese

Maui Wowee Mac & Cheese

High Style Mac & Cheese

Imperial Chicken Mac & Cheese

Tartufo Blanco Mac & Cheese

Fancy Filet Mignon Mac & Cheese

Renaissance Mac & Cheese

Potato, Fennel and Bean Mac & Cheese

Artisan Mac & Cheese

Big Kahuna Mac & Cheese Tuna Bake

Fortune 500 Mac & Cheese

Mac & Cheese Kickin' It Hostel Style
(pages 281 - 292)

Mushroom Mac & Cheese Meatloaf

Champagne Taste Beer Budget

Yelpin' Helpin' Mac & Cheese

Pork, Beans and Burger Mac & Cheese

Mac & Cheese Hash Brown Casserole

Hangover Mac & Cheese

Mac & Cheese Pizza Pie

Cheeseburger Mac & Cheese

Ham and Cauliflower Mac & Cheese

Mac & Cheese Dog Skillet

Bread Bowl Mac & Cheese

Two Four Mac & Cheese

Mac & Cheese Nip

Gone to the Dawgz Mac & Cheese

Mac & Cheese Baked Beans

If I Had a Million Dollars Mac & Cheese

Salt and Vinegar Chips Mac & Cheese

Mac & Cheese BLT

Mac & Cheese Sweet Treats
(pages 293 - 294)

You Bet Your Sweet Mac

Rocky Road Mac & Cheese

Pickles and Ice Cream Mac & Cheese

Attention People, Mr. Mac, Everyday!

For those of you who have some skill in the kitchen or who know how to cook, this cookbook will show you a different way to look at what you can create by simply picking up a box of mac & cheese and considering new ways to prepare it. You and your family will love every meal you prepare from here on forward. Here at the Mac house of cheese we love to cook. It's our goal to get you hooked on the book and cooking too! There's a kid inside of each of us and not only that, when it comes to kids there will be no exceptions – they will discover their ability to pick up this cookbook and become a master Mac man, woman or child. The cooking confidence this book will give you, your kids and your mate will be enormous. You will love the feeling you can get from preparing meals you thought you could never do or even think of.

Watching others create a meal out of what's in the fridge is inspiring. If you can share that feeling with their friends or family, or really with anyone, it gives a sense of accomplishment knowing you just shared a special - "Mac meal!" We are often surprised to see how some cookbooks make cooking look easy. Reading them; however, is a whole other matter - often these cookbooks require a degree in engineering and higher math to figure out what to put in a simple dish. This often puts off aspiring future cooks, especially when the recipes entail a ton of ingredients that you (and most people!) don't have on hand.

Often cookbooks feature recipes that people like the sound of, and the pictures are very seductive, but when it comes to actually cooking the dish we put down the book and search in the fridge or the cupboards for something quick and weasy. Enter mac & cheese - good enough to pass the chef test! This cookbook is designed for everyone who is tired of putting down his or her cookbooks in the hopes of finding something do-able. Every recipe is written in a way that everyone will understand. We are confident that even a noodle head can actually make these recipes themselves. This is a cookbook for all, after all!

Do you have friends coming over for dinner tonight? Don't panic. Grab the mac & cheese! This cookbook will solve the problem of what to make for dinner quickly. Believe me, my mac has gotten me through some tough spots when entertaining in the past. Once you peek through the book and start playing with some food ideas, you will understand why.

Sit back and enjoy the read. No other cookbook will make you feel so hungry! If you didn't have cooking skills before you read this book, look at this as a great opportunity to learn how to boil water and combine ingredients. You will have a happy tummy and a great book to fall back on for any sort of occasion that calls for food.

The
Kenneth Cardell Story

My name is Kenneth (Mac) Cardell and if you will bear with me a bit, I'll tell you a short and (I hope) interesting story about why I call myself the Mac man.

To begin with, I'd like to know how you ended up with this book? Perhaps you were in a rush at the bookstore, or maybe someone dared you to buy it. Maybe you love mac & cheese as much as I do! The good news is, now that you have it, you may as well read my story.

I spent most of my childhood in east Vancouver, British Columbia, my mom was the single mother of seven children and believe me, if you weren't the first one at the table by the time dinner rolled around, well, you just didn't get as much as everyone else. Dinner was a treat at our house and Saturday lunches were the best, we all hung around outside waiting for the hot mac to melt the cheese and then it was chow time.

As soon as I was old enough, I was out working. You name it - I've done it. I was a jack-of-all-trades - a telegram delivery boy for CN/CP, the headstone cleaner at a cemetery, fuel hauler for Esso and produce delivery guy throughout the USA.

I moved around a lot in my younger days so having a trade to settle down to didn't interest me much until I got married. Shortly after getting hitched, my wife and I started a family, we have raised three sons whom have since grown up on mac and are now out on their own.

I was half way through my trucking life when my first son was born in 1981. It was around this time that my buddy Steve and I started up a small company manufacturing disposable cat litter boxes. We named the product "Catch-it." Our product slogan was, "Catch-it in a box or Catch-it in a bag, Catch-it anyway you want to but you better Catch-it!" Three years after we started our company we sold out to a large cat litter supplier from California.

I have been fortunate enough to travel the world many times over, stepping foot in thirty countries - which brings me to now, which is nothing short of a miracle.

In 1997 I made my first trip to Asia in search of new ventures, my first stop was Japan and then on to China. Ever since, I have been hooked on the magic and history of Asia. I moved to China in 1998 and landed in Xiamen, south China. Over the next five years I traveled throughout China and Asia and parts of Europe before moving back to Canada in 2004. To this day I commute back and forth to China buying and selling goods throughout North America. In 2008 I moved to Los Angeles where I lived for two years before winding up back in Vancouver in the fall of 2010.

You may be wondering, "mac & cheese", where does it fit? In fact, mac & cheese fits in every step of my life.

The one thing I always had with me whether at home or travelling was my mac & cheese - and I mean *always*. It is because of mac that I'm writing this story and it is why mac is the focus of this cookbook.

Mac & cheese has been so much a part of my life that people who don't know me wouldn't believe it. I literally packed my bag with mac while I travelled around Asia and Europe, going through customs was always interesting. Believe me, customs officers couldn't believe I had more mac packed in my bags than clothes. Everyone has heard the saying "don't leave home without your American Express card." I often forgot mine, but I was never without my mac.

It's at this point in my life that I want to share with you the many ways you can truly enjoy mac without ever packing your bags – an armchair international "mac & cheese" treat! Pull up a chair, thumb through the book, discover your favorite dish and bring back the kid in you. This cookbook will provide you with 365 unique ways to create a masterpiece fit for a king. I can say that as the self-proclaimed King of Mac, and I'm honored to share my wealth of knowledge about mac & cheese with you. Grab a pot and let's eat!

Mac, Going Way Back

Since I was a little boy I have truly loved my mac to the point of obsession. I simply had to find out more about it. I scoured the net and libraries seeking the truth and now I am pleased to be able to share it with you.

Macaroni and cheese is one of those dishes that nearly everyone seems to love. It is so simple and yet we never tire of it. Rich and creamy with a golden crisp top or dry dressed with ketchup, mac and cheese is the ultimate comfort food, hitting the spot every time. Great for a side dish but also satisfying as meal on its own. Its' simple ingredients makes it a great resource to turn to for a quick meal on a busy day – or a long meal on a slow day. It's always time for some mac & cheese! It also can be easily built upon to invent your own favorite version of the dish and that's exactly why I wrote this special cookbook to share with you.

Macaroni and cheese has been experiencing a bit of a revival over the past couple of years, today we can often spot this dish on menus at trendy restaurants. Let's face it, "mac & cheese" is *cool!* While new versions are fun to taste and almost never disappoint (it's hard to go wrong with butter, cream and cheese), the original will always hold a special place in our hearts.

Ever since the Kraft Company put it in a box in 1937, probably every North American kid has grown up with macaroni and cheese. There is little doubt that its origin was in Italy, were one can find proof of macaroni and cheese recipes from the late thirteenth century. The *Liber de Coquina*, written in Latin by someone familiar with the Neapolitan court that was then under the sphere of Charles II of Anjou (1248-1309), has a recipe called *de lasanis*, which I like to call the first "macaroni and cheese" recipe. It was lasagna sheets made from fermented dough cut into two-inch squares that were cooked in water and tossed with grated cheese, most likely Parmesan. The author suggests using powdered spices and laying the sheets of lasagna, just like today.

The North American "macaroni and cheese" has claims to two main lines of origin, the first is that "macaroni and cheese" was a casserole known as "macaroni pudding" that had its beginnings at a New England church supper. The second and more famous story supports the theory that classic "macaroni and cheese" returned with Thomas Jefferson to Virginia along with a pasta machine after a sojourn in Italy. His daughter, Mary Randolph, who became the hostess of the house after the death of her mother, is who is credited with inventing the dish using macaroni and Parmesan cheese. Later, Parmesan was replaced with Cheddar cheese. My guess is that it is more likely that Jefferson encountered the dish in Italy, had an epiphany and brought back the recipe to share with the rest of the world. Now, let's "mac out!"

Using Mac-365

I am so excited you are here! It's hard to improve on mac & cheese, but we've tried! With Mac-365, you can eat "mac & cheese" a different way every day *for a year*! Or maybe twice a day for about 182 days, or maybe you want to have mac & cheese for every meal? That means you could have a different mac & cheese dish for 122 days! Really, the possibilities are endless.

Here are a few tips to make the most of Mac-365:

Portion size: These recipes are easy to double; just double the portions of every ingredient. The recipes are based on a 200-gram box of your favorite mac & cheese.

Cheese packets: Some of the recipes do not use the cheese packet; save for other uses (see Uses for Cheese Powder).

Seasoning: Many of the herbs and spices called for in Mac-365 are optional… just cook to your taste. If the recipe calls for fresh herbs, dried herbs will work just as well.

Staples: Most of the recipes call for; white onion, garlic, olive oil, salt and pepper, so it's good to have these staples in the kitchen, ready to use.

Equipment: Mac-365 recipes call for either/and: a medium saucepan, a colander, a large skillet, both a large and small mixing bowl, a loaf pan (9"x5"), a large casserole dish (9"x13"), a square casserole dish (9"x9") and/or a large pot (for soups or stews). It's also a good idea to have a set of measuring cups and measuring spoons on hand. Having these items in stock means that you will always be able to whip up a delicious batch of mac & cheese… any time!

Enjoy!

Recipes: Mac-365

Mac & Cheese & What's in the Fridge

From thought to pot to plate: depends what's in your fridge!
Serves: depends what's in your fridge!

Ingredients:

your favorite box of mac & cheese	what's in your fridge... seriously

Cook mac & cheese as directed on the box. Open your fridge, add whatever's in it to your mac & cheese. This is a good way to use up odds and ends such as tomatoes, onions, potatoes, deli meats, leftovers...

Come hungry, leave full! Plus now it's empty, you can give your fridge a good clean!

Appetizers & Soups

Crab Mac and Cheese Mushroom Caps

From thought to pot to plate: 35 minutes

Serves: 6

Ingredients:

box of white Cheddar mac & cheese	2 tablespoons of garlic herb cream cheese
1 can of crab, drained	2 teaspoons of fresh parsley, chopped
salt and pepper to taste	2 dozen mushrooms, stemmed
1 cup of fresh breadcrumbs	¼ cup of Parmesan cheese, grated
1 tablespoon of butter, melted	½ teaspoon of lemon zest
1 clove garlic, minced	

Preheat oven to 350°F. Cook mac & cheese as directed on the box; add cream cheese, crab, salt and pepper. Mix well to combine. Chop mushroom stems and saute in butter with parsley and garlic until tender. Mix into mac and cheese mixture. In small bowl, mix bread crumbs, Parmesan and lemon zest. Arrange caps on a sheet pan and stuff with pasta mixture. Sprinkle with bread crumb topping and bake for 10-12 minutes until heated through and golden brown.

Enjoy!

Macastrone Soup

From thought to pot to plate: 40 minutes
Serves: 2

Ingredients:

your favorite box of mac & cheese	2 tablespoons of olive oil
2 cloves of garlic, minced	½ cup of white onion, diced
2 medium carrots, peeled, chopped	2 large celery stalks, chopped
1 can of tomatoes, not drained	2 tablespoons of tomato paste
1 cup of water	3 cups of vegetable stock
1 can of pinto beans rinsed and drained	1 tablespoon of fresh basil, chopped

Heat oil in large stockpot over medium heat; sauté garlic and onion until soft. Add carrots and celery and sauté for 5 minutes. Next add tomatoes, paste, water and vegetable stock; bring to a boil then cook on medium, uncovered for 5 minutes. Add pasta (*reserve cheese for another use*); boil uncovered until macaroni is tender. Turn heat to low, add beans; stir until heated through. Garnish with basil. Serve.

Buon appetito!

Noodle Notes: ....
....
....
....
....
....
....
....
....
....
....
....

Mac & Cheese Bruschetta

From thought to pot to plate: 45 minutes

Serves: 8

Ingredients:

your favorite box of mac & cheese	1 loaf of thick French bread, sliced
5 large tomatoes, chopped	½ cup of fresh parsley, chopped
salt and pepper to taste	3 cloves of garlic, minced
½ cup of Parmesan, grated	½ cup of white onion, diced
dash of olive oil	1 teaspoon of balsamic vinegar
½ cup of fresh basil, chopped	2 cups of mozzarella cheese, grated

Preheat oven to 350°F. Cook mac & cheese as directed on the box. In a bowl, combine the tomatoes, parsley, salt, pepper, garlic, Parmesan, onion and olive oil. Set in the refrigerator for about half an hour for the flavors to blend. Slice the French bread on a bias. Place on large sheet pan and place a spoonful of mac & cheese on each, followed by a spoonful of the chilled bruschetta mixture. Top with the mozzarella cheese and bake for about 15 minutes or until bubbling and the tops are golden brown. Serve hot, garnished with fresh basil and a drizzle of balsamic vinegar.

Enjoy!

Noodle Notes: ....

....

....

....

....

....

....

....

....

Mac & Cheese with Pico de Gallo

From thought to pot to plate: 45 minutes

Serves: 4

Ingredients:

your favorite box of mac & cheese	dash of olive oil
½ cup of white onion, diced	1 cup of mushrooms, sliced
1½ teaspoon of chili powder	½ teaspoon of cumin
1½ cup of Monterey Jack cheese, grated	1 can of black beans, drained
1 large tomato, chopped	½ cup of red onion, diced
½ cup of jalapenos, diced	2 tablespoons of fresh cilantro, chopped
1 teaspoon of fresh squeezed lime juice	¼ teaspoon of kosher salt

Prepare pico de gallo by combining the tomato, red onion, jalapenos, cilantro, lime juice and salt; set aside for the flavors to develop. Cook mac & cheese as directed on the box. In a skillet, heat olive oil over medium high heat; add onion, mushroom, chili powder and cumin cook for about 5-7 minutes; stir frequently. Add cheese and stir until melted, then lower heat and put prepared mac & cheese and black beans into the skillet. Combine and heat through. Top each serving with pico de gallo and enjoy!

Olé!

Pesto Mac & Feta Portobello Caps

From thought to pot to plate: 45 minutes

Serves: 6

Ingredients:

your favorite box of mac & cheese	¾ cup of feta cheese, crumbled
¾ cup of pesto (Recipes Reference)	salt and pepper to taste
6 large Portobello mushrooms, stemmed	

Preheat oven to 375°F. Cook mac & cheese as directed on the box. In a medium sized bowl, mix feta with pesto; season with salt and pepper. Set cleaned mushrooms upside down on a sheet pan, place mac & cheese on top followed by feta and pesto mixture. Bake for 10 minutes or until bubbling and golden brown.

Awesome on a burger! Enjoy!

Mac & Cheese Poppers

From thought to pot to plate: 45 minutes

Serves: 4

Ingredients:

your favorite box of mac & cheese	1 cup of flour
1 tablespoon of cornstarch	1½ cups of seltzer water
frying oil	pickled jalapenos, sliced

Cook mac & cheese as directed on the box; set in the refrigerator to chill and set. To make tempura batter, combine the flour, cornstarch and seltzer water in a bowl. Scoop spoonfuls of mac & cheese one by one and coat with batter. Drop in hot oil. Once cooked, drain on a paper towel and serve with jalapenos.

Enjoy!

Na' Cho Average Mac & Cheese

From thought to pot to plate: 35 minutes
Serves: 2

Ingredients:

your favorite box of mac & cheese	½ lb. of lean ground beef
1 package of tortilla chips	3 green onions, sliced
½ cup of red onion, diced	1 can of sliced black olives, drained
1 cup of Cheddar cheese, grated	1 large tomato, chopped
salsa, as garnish	sour cream, as garnish
1 avocado, sliced	

Preheat oven to 350°F. Cook mac & cheese as directed on the box. Cook the ground beef in a skillet. In a high-sided sheet pan place a layer of tortilla chips. Layer a bit of mac & cheese, beef, green onion, red onion, olives, cheese and tomato, and repeat again with a layer of tortillas, then the other ingredients. Bake in the oven for about 7 minutes or until the cheese melts. Serve with sides of salsa, sour cream and avocado.

Serve with a round of pops and instant celebrity status!

Noodle Notes: ....

....

....

....

....

....

....

....

....

....

....

Mac-erranean Dip

From thought to pot to plate: 35 minutes
Serves: 4

Ingredients:

your favorite box of mac & cheese	1 cup of feta cheese, crumbled
4 marinated artichoke hearts, chopped	½ cup green olives, pitted
½ cup sour cream	1 teaspoon of olive oil
1 teaspoon of fresh basil, chopped	1 teaspoon of dried oregano
1 clove of garlic, minced	2 teaspoons of fresh lemon juice

Cook mac & cheese as directed on the box. Place all other ingredients in a food processor or mix by hand till almost smooth and combine with the mac & cheese. Great with pita chips or sliced French bread.

Enjoy!

Angels on Horseback Mac & Cheese

From thought to pot to plate: 35 minutes
Serves 8

Ingredients:

your favorite box of mac & cheese	1 can of smoked oysters, drained
8 slices of bacon, raw	2 tablespoons of fresh parsley, chopped
1/8 teaspoon of paprika	2 limes, cut into wedges
salt and pepper to taste	

Cook mac & cheese as directed on the box. In a heated skillet, partially cook the sliced bacon and set aside to cool and drain on a paper towel. Preheat the broiler. Wrap each oyster with half a slice of bacon (with overlap), secure with a toothpick and place on a sheet pan. Sprinkle with salt, pepper, paprika and parsley. Bake for about 10 minutes and serve immediately with a squeeze of lime on a bed of mac & cheese.

You know what they say about what happens when you eat oysters…

Addie's Nibbles

From thought to pot to plate: 60 minutes
Serves: 4

Ingredients:

your favorite box of mac & cheese	½ cup of Gruyere cheese, grated
½ cup of mozzarella cheese, grated	1 egg, beaten
¼ cup of mayonnaise	1 teaspoon of lemon juice
½ cup of milk	salt and pepper to taste
oil for frying	½ cup of flour
1 cup of French-fried onions, crushed	1 cup of breadcrumbs
2 eggs, beaten	

Cook mac & cheese as directed on the box; add the Gryere and mozzarella and combine. In another bowl combine eggs, mayonnaise, lemon juice, milk, salt and pepper; add to the mac & cheese and chill for at least 45 minutes. Cut the chilled mac & cheese mixture into bite-sized squares. Heat 2" of oil in a heavy pan. Dredge each square in flour, then egg, followed by breadcrumbs and crushed French-fried onions to coat. Fry in hot oil for 1 minute a side or until golden brown. Drain on paper towels before serving.

Enjoy!

Mac & Cheese French Onion Soup

From thought to pot to plate: 70 minutes

Serves: 4

Ingredients:

your favorite box of mac & cheese	8 large white onions, thinly sliced
2 sprigs of fresh thyme	1 cup of water
1 - 900ml carton of beef broth	1 bottle of pale ale
3 tablespoons of butter	salt and pepper to taste
1 tablespoon of Worcestershire sauce	4 thin slices of French bread, toasted
1 cup of Swiss cheese, grated	

Cook mac & cheese as directed on the box. In a large stockpot, heat onions in melted butter for about one minute, followed by water and thyme. Cook covered on medium high heat for about 35 minutes, stirring often, until the liquid is reduced. Remove the thyme. When the liquid has evaporated, remove the lid, turn heat on low and caramelize the onions, stirring frequently for about 20 minutes. Once the onions are golden and soft, add the broth, Worcestershire sauce and beer and let simmer for about 10 minutes. Ladle soup into ovenproof bowls on a sheet pan. Fit a slice of toasted French bread into the top of each bowl, topped with a spoonful of mac & cheese and sprinkled evenly with Swiss cheese. Place under the broiler until soup is bubbling and the tops are golden brown.

Bon appétit!

Mac & Cheese Seven Layer Dip

From thought to pot to plate: 45 minutes

Serves: 6

Ingredients:

your favorite box of mac & cheese	package of taco seasoning mix (35 g.)
1 can of refried beans	1 small jar of salsa
1 small container of sour cream	1 large tomato, chopped
1 bunch of green onions, sliced	2 avocados, sliced
2 cups of iceberg lettuce, shredded	1 can of sliced black olives, drained
2 cups of Cheddar cheese, grated	½ cup of fresh cilantro, chopped
tortilla chips	

Cook mac & cheese as directed on the box. Put in the refrigerator to chill. Prepare the taco seasoning as directed on the package and combine with the mac & cheese and sour cream. In a flat-bottomed bowl or casserole dish, layer the taco seasoning/sour cream mac & cheese mixture, followed by a layer of refried beans, chopped avocadoes, then tomato mixed with salsa, green onions and iceberg lettuce, black olives and Cheddar cheese. Garnish with cilantro. Serve chilled with tortilla chips.

Mac 365 secret: This dish will keep you busy on the social circuit!

Cheddar Cheese Soup

From thought to pot to plate: 40 minutes

Serves: 6

Ingredients:

¼ cup of Cheddar cheese powder	2 tablespoons of butter
1 cup of celery, chopped	½ cup of white onion, diced
1 cup of parsnip, chopped	2 carrots, peeled and chopped
2 cloves of garlic, minced	2 teaspoons of thyme, chopped
4 cups of vegetable broth	2 tablespoons of cornstarch
¼ cup of cold water	1 cup of Cheddar cheese, grated
¾ cup of half and half	salt and pepper to taste
dash of hot sauce	

In a stockpot, melt butter; add celery and onions and cook until onions are translucent. Add parsnips, carrots, garlic, thyme and vegetable broth; simmer for 10-15 minutes until vegetables are tender. Dissolve the cornstarch in water and stir in to thicken along with the cheese powder, grated cheese and half and half. Stir until cheese is melted; add hot sauce and salt and pepper to taste. Puree with a hand blender or stand mixer.

Enjoy!

Mac 'n' Eggs

Mac & Cheese Meat Lover's Eggs Strata

From thought to pot to plate: 70 minutes
Serves: 4

Ingredients:

your favorite box of mac & cheese	1 cup of croutons
2 Italian chorizo sausages	½ cup of pancetta, chopped
1 cup of zucchini, chopped	½ cup of red pepper, diced
½ cup of red onion, diced	1 cup of white Cheddar, grated
1 teaspoon of dried parsley	8 eggs, beaten
½ teaspoon of dry mustard	1 cup of light cream
salt and pepper to taste	1 teaspoon of butter

Preheat oven to 350°F. Cook mac & cheese as directed on the box. Spread croutons and mac & cheese evenly in the bottom of a greased casserole dish and set aside. In a large skillet, cook the chorizo (with casings removed) and pancetta until crispy; remove from heat and place on paper towel to drain. Cook the zucchini, onion, parsley, mustard and red pepper until soft. Spoon both the meat mixture and the vegetables evenly over the mac & cheese. In a separate bowl, whisk together the eggs, light cream, salt and pepper. Pour egg mixture evenly over sausage, pancetta and vegetables. Let the casserole stand for about 10 minutes before baking. Top with Cheddar and bake for about 50 minutes or until bubbling and the top is golden brown. Let stand for 10 minutes before serving.

Enjoy!

Blue Plate Special Mac & Cheese

From thought to pot to plate: 25 minutes
Serves: 2

Ingredients:

your favorite box of mac & cheese	1 green onion, sliced
4 eggs	6 strips of bacon
salt and pepper to taste	

Cook mac & cheese as directed on the box. Place bacon in a mid-sized skillet and cook until crisp, set aside on a paper towel to drain. Drain most of the bacon fat from pan. Whisk together eggs, green onion, salt and pepper; add to pan to cook. Serve with a side of mac & cheese with bacon.

This will surpass all of your egg-spectations!

Mac & Cheese Waffles

From thought to pot to plate: 55 minutes
Serves: 2

Ingredients:

your favorite box of mac & cheese	2 eggs, beaten
¾ cup of flour	dash of salt
½ cup of panko breadcrumbs	

Cook mac & cheese as directed on the box. Spread mixture on a sheet pan and refrigerate for about 45 minutes. Once set, cut into waffle sized pieces; dredge in flour with a dash of salt in it, then in egg, followed by the panko. Place in hot greased waffle iron and cook until golden brown on both sides. Serve with syrup, macerated strawberries, whatever!

Hey, why not?

Quiche à la Mac et Fromage

From thought to pot to plate: 45 minutes
Serves: 2

Ingredients:

your favorite box of spiral mac & cheese	dash of olive oil
½ cup of white onion, diced	½ cup of green pepper, chopped
½ cup of cooked ham, cubed	7 eggs, beaten
¼ cup of plain yogurt	salt and pepper to taste
½ cup of Monterey Jack cheese, grated	2 tablespoons of fresh parsley, chopped

Preheat oven to 350°F. Cook mac & cheese as directed on the box. Heat the olive oil in a large skillet over medium heat. Add the onion and green pepper and cook until soft; add the chopped ham and cook for another minute. In a large mixing bowl beat eggs and combine with plain yogurt. Add the prepared mac & cheese, cheese, salt, pepper and parsley to the skillet and combine. Pour the egg mixture over everything and put the skillet in the oven, bake for about 40 minutes or until set.

Have an egg-cellent day!

Noodle Notes:

Bacon and Eggs Mac & Cheese

From thought to pot to plate: 45 minutes

Serves: 2

Ingredients:

your favorite box of mac & cheese	6 slices of bacon
4 eggs	½ cup of Cheddar cheese, grated
salt and pepper to taste	½ cup of breadcrumbs
1 teaspoon of dried parsley	

Cook mac & cheese as directed on the box. Cook bacon slices in a skillet until crispy and set aside on paper towel to drain. In the same skillet, cook the breadcrumbs and parsley until crispy and set aside. To assemble, spread half the mac and cheese in a greased casserole dish and top with bacon, follow with remaining pasta. In the skillet cook the eggs sunny side up, and put on the second layer of the mac & cheese, covered by the crispy breadcrumbs and parsley mixture. Serve.

Why have just bacon and eggs when you can have bacon and eggs mac & cheese?

Noodle Notes: ....
....
....
....
....
....
....
....
....
....
....
....

Mac & Cheese French Toast

From thought to pot to plate: 50 minutes
Serves: 4

Ingredients:

your favorite box of mac & cheese	8 slices of your favorite bread
6 eggs	dash of salt
1 tablespoon of butter	

Cook mac & cheese as directed on the box. Place in a loaf pan and put in refrigerator to set for about 40 minutes. Once set, slice four pieces of it, much like bread, to your desired thickness. Combine the eggs and salt in a medium sized bowl. Place slices of mac & cheese between slices of bread (sandwich style) and dip in egg mixture to coat. In a medium hot skillet sizzling with melted butter, place your coated "sandwiches" to cook until golden brown. Serve with side condiment such as hot sauce, HP sauce or ketchup.

* For a sweet version, add a pinch of cinnamon and a dash of vanilla to the egg mixture and serve with maple syrup instead.

This will get people out of bed on weekends!

Noodle Notes: ....

....

....

....

....

....

....

....

....

....

....

BMB Mac & Cheese Quiche

From thought to pot to plate: 55 minutes

Serves: 2

Ingredients:

your favorite box of mac & cheese	1 - 12" piecrust, unbaked
½ cup of fresh mushrooms, sliced	1 cup of broccoli florets
4 slices of bacon, chopped	1 cup of mozzarella, grated
4 eggs, beaten	1 cup of heavy cream
salt and pepper to taste	½ cup of white onion, diced
¼ cup of fresh parsley, chopped	¾ teaspoon of paprika

Preheat oven to 400°F. Cook mac & cheese as directed on the box. In a large skillet, cook the chopped bacon until crispy and set aside on paper towel to drain; and then sauté the onion, mushrooms and broccoli until soft. In a separate bowl, combine cream, eggs, mozzarella, parsley and paprika; add onion, mushroom broccoli mixture with bacon and one cup of mac & cheese. Salt and pepper to taste. Stir to combine and pour into piecrust. Bake for 15 minutes, then turn down to 325°F and bake for another 40 minutes or until set.

Use the leftover mac and add to scrambled eggs with green onions for breakfast!

Mac & Cheese Bacon Broccoli Frittata

From thought to pot to plate: 45 minutes
Serves: 2

Ingredients:

your favorite box of mac & cheese	5 eggs, beaten
salt and pepper to taste	1 teaspoon of butter
1 cup of Cheddar cheese, grated	3 slices of bacon, chopped
½ cup of broccoli florets	½ cup of red onion, sliced
¼ cup of milk	1 cup of breadcrumbs
2 tablespoons of fresh parsley, chopped	

Preheat oven to 350°F. Cook mac & cheese as directed on the box. Beat eggs with the milk, salt and pepper and set aside. Heat a large skillet over medium heat and cook the bacon until crispy; then set aside on paper towel to drain. Wipe skillet clean. Melt butter in the pan and cook onion and broccoli until soft, then add the egg mixture, bacon and half of the mac & cheese, topped with Cheddar cheese and breadcrumbs. Let cook for about 4 minutes, then place skillet in the oven to finish the frittata - until the breadcrumbs are golden brown, the cheese is melted and the eggs are set. Remove and let cool for about 3 minutes before loosening and sliding onto a cutting board or serving plate. Cut into wedges and garnish with parsley.

Perfect for breakfast, lunch or dinner!

Mile High City Mac & Cheese

From thought to pot to plate: 40 minutes
Serves: 2

Ingredients:

your favorite box of mac & cheese	5 large eggs, beaten
½ cup of white onion, diced	½ cup of red peppers, seeded and diced
½ cup of green peppers, diced	½ cup of cooked ham, cubed
3 slices of bacon, chopped	½ cup of fresh mushrooms, sliced
salt and pepper to taste	1 teaspoon of butter

Cook mac & cheese as directed on the box. Cook the bacon until crispy; set aside on a paper towel to drain. Sauté onions, peppers and mushrooms in butter until soft, then add ham. In a small bowl, beat the eggs and salt and pepper together. Slowly stir the eggs into the mixture in the skillet, along with the bacon and a cup of mac & cheese. Lightly brown on one side, then turn over and lightly brown the other, flip and serve.

Now you can have leftover mac & cheese for dinner – hurrah!

Noodle Notes: ....
....
....
....
....
....
....
....
....
....
....
....

Mac 'n' Greens

Antipasto Mac & Cheese

From thought to pot to plate: 45 minutes
Serves: 4

Ingredients:

your favorite box of mac & cheese	1 can of tuna, drained
¾ cup of red wine vinegar	¼ cup of packed brown sugar
2 tablespoons of Worcestershire sauce	salt and pepper to taste
1 can of tomato paste	2 teaspoons of hot sauce
½ cup of green beans, in ½" pieces	½ cup of cauliflower, cut into florets
½ cup of red onion, chopped	½ cup red pepper, chopped
½ cup of zucchini, peeled and chopped	½ cup of carrots, peeled, chopped
½ cup of celery, chopped	½ cup of green olives, pitted
3 cloves of garlic, minced	1 teaspoon of oregano
1 small fennel bulb, chopped	1 small jar of marinated artichoke hearts

Cook mac & cheese as directed on the box, then chill in the refrigerator. In a large saucepan combine the vinegar, sugar, Worcestershire sauce, salt, paste and hot pepper sauce. Stir occasionally; bring to a boil. Add the beans, cauliflower, fennel, onion, red peppers, zucchini, celery and garlic and cook until vegetables are softened – about five minutes. Add the olives, drained artichokes, oregano and tuna. Combine and chill mixture. Serve folded into the cold mac & cheese with crackers or sliced French bread.

Enjoy!

Mac & Cheese Chicken Salad

From thought to pot to plate: 30 minutes

Ingredients:

your favorite box of mac & cheese	1 cup cooked chicken breast, cubed
½ cup of celery, chopped	½ cup of red pepper, chopped
½ cup red onion, diced	¾ cup of mayonnaise
salt and pepper to taste	

Cook mac & cheese as directed on the box. Combine with the remaining ingredients in a bowl and chill before serving.

Easy, eh?

MacaRoma Salad

From thought to pot to plate: 45 minutes
Serves: 2

Ingredients:

your favorite box of mac & cheese	¼ cup of olive oil mayonnaise
1 teaspoon of Italian salad dressing	½ cup of marinated artichoke hearts
¾ cup grape tomatoes, halved	½ cup of canned sliced black olives
½ cup of baby bocconcini cheese	¼ cup of fresh oregano, chopped

Cook mac & cheese as directed on the box *without the cheese packet*. Drain and rinse macaroni in cold water. Mix cheese packet with the mayonnaise and salad dressing and stir into cooked pasta. Add drained and quartered artichoke hearts, grape tomatoes, olives, chopped cheese and oregano. Stir to combine. Cover and refrigerate before serving.

Enjoy!

Mac & Cheese Salad Nicoise

From thought to pot to plate: 45 minutes

Serves: 4

Ingredients:

---

your favorite box of mac & cheese

vinaigrette:

2 tablespoons of apple cider vinegar

1 tablespoon of grainy mustard

½ cup of olive oil

1 white onion, sliced thinly

2 cloves of garlic, minced

2 cups of parsley, chopped

1 cup of fresh tarragon, chopped

salt and pepper to taste

salad:

2 cans of tuna, preferably oil packed

1 head of Boston lettuce

½ lb. of green beans, trimmed

½ lb. of yellow beans, trimmed

1lb. of new potatoes, scrubbed

½ red pepper, chopped

½ yellow pepper, chopped

4 tomatoes, quartered

4 eggs, hard-boiled, quartered

1 cup of Nicoise olives

1 shallot, diced

1 can of anchovy fillets, drained

3 tablespoons of capers

Cook mac & cheese as directed on the box. Make vinaigrette by whisking the vinegar and mustard in a bowl. Stir in the garlic, onions, parsley and tarragon, then season with salt and pepper. Place beans over boiling water and steam for approximately 5 minutes until tender; remove and set aside to cool. Add potatoes to steamer and cook until tender; about 15 minutes. Rinse potatoes under cold water to cool quickly, drain and quarter. Add beans and potatoes to vinaigrette in bowl; stir gently to combine. On a large platter plate the mac and cheese; add the chopped lettuce and top with bean and potato mixture, tuna, anchovies, eggs, tomatoes, shallots, capers and olives. Drizzle the platter with remaining vinaigrette and garnish with parsley.

Fancy eh? This is my tea party mac & cheese.

Mac & Cheese Pasta Salad with Salami

From thought to pot to plate: 45 minutes

Serves: 2

Ingredients:

your favorite box of mac & cheese	dash of olive oil
1 red pepper, chopped	½ cup of red onion, diced
1 small eggplant, cubed	5oz. of salami, in bite-sized pieces
1 jar of tomato sauce	1 tablespoon of parsley, chopped
¼ cup of Parmesan cheese, grated	salt and pepper to taste

Cook mac & cheese as directed on the box. Heat oil in a frying pan; add peppers, onion, eggplant and salami and cook until tender. Add tomato sauce and parsley and stir until heated through. Add vegetable mixture to the prepared mac & cheese, stir to combine and serve topped with Parmesan. Serve hot or cold.

Who says you can't cook?

Noodle Notes: ....
....
....
....
....
....
....
....
....
....
....
....
....

Mac & Cheese Rainbow Salad

From thought to pot to plate: 40 minutes

Serves: 4

Ingredients:

your favorite box of mac & cheese	1 cup of plain yogurt
½ cup of mayonnaise	1 tablespoon of lemon juice
salt and pepper	½ cup of red onion, diced
2 green onions, sliced	1 teaspoon of fresh dill, chopped
1½ cup of frozen corn niblets, thawed	1½ cup of broccoli, cut into florets
6 tomatoes, chopped	1½ cups of red cabbage, shredded
1½ cups of orange pepper, diced	

Cook mac & cheese as directed on the box; set aside to cool in the refrigerator. In a large jar with lid, combine yogurt, mayonnaise, lemon juice, onions, dill, salt and pepper. Seal and shake to mix; place in refrigerator to chill. When ready to serve; arrange vegetables in bands of color on a large serving platter. Start with tomatoes, orange pepper, chilled mac & cheese, corn, broccoli, end with cabbage. Cover and chill for about an hour before serving with the side of dressing.

Enjoy!

Noodle Notes: ....
....
....
....
....
....
....
....
....
....

Mac & Cheese Waldolf Salad

From thought to pot to plate: 45 minutes

Serves: 2

Ingredients:

your favorite box of mac & cheese	2 granny smith apples, chopped
1 teaspoon of lemon juice	1 cup of seedless green grapes, halved
2 stalks of celery, chopped	2 green onions, sliced
1 tablespoon of mayonnaise	2 tablespoons of plain yogurt
1 tablespoon of apple juice	½ teaspoon of celery seed, ground
1 cup of walnuts, crumbled	1 bunch of watercress, chopped
salt and pepper to taste	

Cook mac & cheese as directed on the box; set in the refrigerator to cool. In a large bowl, combine the peeled, cored and chopped apples and lemon juice. Add the grapes, celery and green onions. In second bowl, whisk together the yogurt, mayonnaise, apple juice, celery seed, salt and pepper. Combine with the apple mixture and fold gently. On a platter arrange cleaned watercress on a bed of chilled mac & cheese; with the apple mixture on top and sprinkle with crumbled walnuts. Refrigerate for an hour before serving.

Your guests will want to wear cravats to eat this!

Smoked Salmon Mac & Cheese Salad

From thought to pot to plate: 30 minutes
Serves: 2

Ingredients:

box of mac & white Cheddar cheese	1 cup of smoked salmon, chopped
1 cup of cooked frozen peas, thawed	2 stalks of celery, sliced
4 green onions, sliced	1 tablespoon of fresh dill, chopped
1 tablespoon of pepper	½ cup of mayonnaise
juice of one lemon	

Cook mac & cheese as directed on the box. Let cool. In a small bowl combine dill, mayonnaise, lemon juice and dill and set aside. Place the pasta in large bowl; add salmon, peas, celery, green onions with the mayonnaise mixture; stir to combine and chill to serve.

Enjoy!

Noodle Notes: ....

....

....

....

....

....

....

....

....

....

....

....

Mac & Cheese Coleslaw

From thought to pot to plate: 35 minutes

Serves: 4

Ingredients:

your favorite box of mac & cheese	¼ head of white cabbage, thinly sliced
¼ head of red cabbage, thinly sliced	½ cup of red onion, diced
2 carrots, peels and grated	1 cup of fresh cilantro, chopped
3 green onions, sliced	1 jalapeno pepper, diced
1 clove of garlic, minced	juice of one lime
½ teaspoon of celery salt	2 teaspoons of grainy mustard
2 tablespoons of mayonnaise	1 tablespoon of white vinegar
salt and pepper to taste	

Cook mac & cheese as directed on the box. Cool slightly and add the remaining ingredients. Serve cold.

Enjoy!

Noodle Notes: ....

....

....

....

....

....

....

....

....

....

....

....

Cobb Mac & Cheese Salad

From thought to pot to plate: 40 minutes

Serves: 4

Ingredients:

your favorite box of mac & cheese	6 slices of bacon, chopped
4 eggs, boiled and peeled	dash of olive oil
1 head of iceberg lettuce, shredded	2 chicken breasts, in bite-sized pieces
2 tomatoes, diced	1 cup of blue cheese, crumbled
2 avocados, sliced	4 green onions, sliced
4 tablespoons of Ranch-style dressing	salt and pepper to taste
1 teaspoon of lemon juice	

Cook mac & cheese as directed on the box and set in refrigerator to cool. Cook the chicken in the skillet, remove from heat and place in refrigerator to cool. Cook bacon in a skillet until crispy and then set aside on paper towel to drain. Crumble and set aside. Divide shredded lettuce among individual plates, followed by the chicken, tomatoes, blue cheese, bacon, mac & cheese, sliced eggs, avocado and green onions to garnish. Drizzle salad with lemon juice, add dressing and serve.

Enjoy!

Deli Mac & Cheese Salad

From thought to pot to plate: 60 minutes
Serves: 2

Ingredients:

your favorite box of mac & cheese	5 oz. jar of roasted red peppers, chopped
5 oz. of sun-dried tomatoes, chopped	5 oz. of canned black olives, sliced
5 oz. of salami, cut into strips	½ cup of fresh basil leaves, chopped
½ cup of Italian dressing	2 tablespoons of pesto (Recipes Reference)

Cook mac & cheese as directed on the box. Combine and fresh basil, Italian dressing and pesto in a jar and shake well. Place pasta and dressing in large bowl with remaining ingredients and toss to combine. Refrigerate for an hour to combine the flavors.

Enjoy!

Spring Fling Mac & Cheese Salad

From thought to pot to plate: 25 minutes
Serves: 2

Ingredients:

box of mac & white cheddar cheese	1 bunch of asparagus tips, steamed
1 cup of cooked ham, cubed	1 teaspoon fresh dill, chopped
salt and pepper to taste	

Cook mac & cheese as directed on the box. Add asparagus and cooked ham. Mix together with a sprinkle of fresh dill. Add salt and pepper to taste. Serve chilled.

Enjoy!

Mac & Cheese Three Bean Salad

From thought to pot to plate: 45 minutes
Serves: 4

Ingredients:

your favorite box of mac & cheese	1 cup of green beans, chopped
1 can of kidney beans, drained	1 can of garbanzo beans, drained
1 cup of parsley, chopped	juice of one lemon
½ cup of red onion, diced	3 green onions, sliced
3 cloves of garlic, minced	1 teaspoon of white vinegar
½ cup of fresh cilantro, chopped	2 teaspoons of olive oil
salt and pepper to taste	

Cook mac & cheese as directed on the box; set in the refrigerator to cool. Cook the green beans in boiling water until tender, then rinse in cold water to cool. In a large bowl, combine the rinsed beans, parsley, lemon juice, red onion, green onion, garlic, vinegar, cilantro, olive oil, salt and pepper together; then mix with the mac & cheese. Serve cold.

Enjoy!

Noodle Notes: ....

....

....

....

....

....

....

....

....

....

Mac & Cheese Peach Salad

From thought to pot to plate: 30 minutes

Serves: 2

Ingredients:

box of mac & white Cheddar cheese	1 tablespoon of canola oil
2 stalks of celery, sliced	½ cup of white onion, diced
1 clove of garlic, minced	1 red pepper, diced
1½ teaspoons of garam masala	1 - 14 oz. can of peaches in natural juice
½ cup of mayonnaise	½ cup of green grapes
salt and pepper to taste	½ cup of pecans, crumbled

Cook mac & cheese as directed on the box. Melt butter in a heated skillet; sauté celery, onion, garlic and peppers until soft. Add garam masala and cook for another 2 minutes. Remove mixture from heat and set aside. Open the can of peaches, drain and reserve the juice. Cut the peaches into bite-sized pieces and add to the skillet and stir to combine, along with the grapes; then add the peach juice. In a casserole dish combine the mac & cheese, peppers, onion, peach mixture and mayonnaise, season with salt and pepper and refrigerate until chilled. When ready to serve, sprinkle with chopped pecans.

Healthy healthy healthy!

Mac & Cheese Caesar Salad

From thought to pot to plate: 35 minutes
Serves: 4

Ingredients:

your favorite box of mac & cheese	1 head of romaine lettuce, chopped
½ cup of pancetta, chopped	2 cloves of garlic, minced
salt and pepper to taste	3 tablespoons of olive oil
1 teaspoon of Worcestershire sauce	1 teaspoon of anchovy paste
1 teaspoon of capers	1/3 cup of Parmesan cheese, grated
1 teaspoon of Dijon mustard	juice of one lemon
1 tablespoon of mayonnaise	1 tablespoon of butter
1 cup of panko breadcrumbs	1 egg, beaten
½ cup of flour	

Cook mac & cheese as directed on the box; then put in the refrigerator to chill. Combine minced garlic and anchovies and place in a large bowl. Squeeze in 2 tablespoons of lemon juice. Add Dijon, Worcestershire, salt and pepper. Whisk to combine. Gradually add the olive oil and mayonnaise to emulsify, with about half of the Parmesan. Cook pancetta until crispy; set aside on a paper towel to drain. Combine lettuce, pancetta, dressing and remaining Parmesan and the rest of the lemon juice. For croutons, dredge a small scoop of cold mac & cheese in flour, the egg, then panko and cook in melted butter. Repeat until you have enough "croutons" for your salad.

Enjoy!

Mac Du Canada

Canuck Mac & Cheese

From thought to pot to plate: 40 minutes

Serves: 2

Ingredients:

your favorite box of mac & cheese	1 cup of Canadian Cheddar, grated
3 tablespoons of Canadian maple syrup	1 clove of garlic, minced
½ cup of parsley, chopped	1 teaspoon of butter
1 cup of breadcrumbs	6 slices of Canadian bacon, chopped
½ cup of red onion, diced	

Preheat oven to 350°F. Cook mac & cheese as directed on the box. Fry bacon in a skillet until crispy and transfer to a paper towel to drain; then cook red onion until translucent. In a separate pan, melt the butter and add breadcrumbs and parsley. Stir to combine until crispy. Combine the mac & cheese, onions, bacon and maple syrup in a greased casserole dish. Top with breadcrumb mixture and Cheddar cheese. Bake for about 15 minutes or until bubbling and the top is golden brown. Let stand for 10 minutes before serving.

Those Canucks sure are sophisticated!

British Columbia: Wet Coast Mac & Cheese

From thought to pot to plate: 35 minutes
Serves: 2

Ingredients:

your favorite box of mac & cheese	1 Dungeness crab, in shell
1/4 cup of butter, melted	3 cloves of garlic, minced
thimble full of your favorite tipple	salt and pepper to taste

Cook mac & cheese as directed on the box. Boil a pot of water deep enough to cover the crab. Once boiling, throw the crab in. Cook approximately 7 minutes or until the shell is pink. Remove the crab from the water and set aside to cool; once cool, remove the shell. Heat butter and add garlic, sauté until light brown; then throw in vodka, salt and pepper and heat until warm. Pour mixture over the crab and combine with mac & cheese.

Now I know why this is the coast with the most, and you can be the host with the most

Quebec: Mon Dieu Mac & Cheese

From thought to pot to plate: 15 minutes or 2 hours
(depending where you get your poutine!)
Serves: 2

Ingredients:

your favorite box of mac & cheese	poutine from your favorite depanneur
pepper to taste	

Cook mac & cheese as directed on the box. Combine all of the above. Bid your diet adieu.

Slip slidin' away into bud-tasty Poutineville. Oh là là. C'est formidable!

Alberta: Home on the Range Mac & Cheese

From thought to pot to plate: 30 minutes
Serves: 2

Ingredients:

your favorite box of mac & cheese	1 bison rib eye steak
1/2 cup of Cheddar cheese, grated	1/2 green pepper, diced
½ cup of white onion, diced	dash of olive oil
dash of cayenne pepper	salt and pepper to taste

Cook mac & cheese as directed on the box. Heat oil in a skillet and sauté the green pepper and onion. Cut bison steak into cubes; add to the frying pan and cook to your liking. Add a dash of cayenne pepper and salt and pepper to taste. Add the grated cheddar cheese on top and let it melt. Mix in the mac & cheese or serve sidesaddle.

Oh give me a home, where the buffalo roam, and the mac and the cheese come to play…

Saskatchewan: Wheat - Treat Mac & Cheese

From thought to pot to plate: 15 minutes
Serves: 2

Ingredients:

your favorite box of *whole-wheat* mac & cheese	perogies (a prairie favorite)
or sweet and sour pork (a prairie favorite)	

Cook mac & cheese as directed on the box. Add optional perogies or sweet and sour pork, found in most Saskatchewan towns from Fond-du-Lac to Weyburn.

Hey where did the noodles come from? Don't tell me the grain elevator!

Manitoba: Golden Boy Mac & Cheese

From thought to pot to plate: 15 minutes
Serves: 2

Ingredients:

your favorite box of mac & cheese	1 smoked Goldeye, chilled
salt and pepper to taste	

Cook mac & cheese as directed on the box. Serve chilled Goldeye on the side; salt and pepper to taste.

Who is that naked boy running around with the fish in his hand? Who cares? Let's eat!

Ontario: Drive By the Lake Mac & Cheese

From thought to pot to plate: 30 minutes
Serves: 2

Ingredients:

your favorite box of mac & cheese	1lb. of fresh water pickerel
1 cup of flour	dash of cayenne pepper
salt and pepper to taste	dash of olive oil

Cook mac & cheese as directed on the box. Combine flour, cayenne pepper, salt and pepper and coat the pickerel in the mix. Heat olive oil in a frying pan. Once hot, add the coated fish. Cook approximately three minutes per side, flipping once. Serve with mac & cheese.

What lake was that, baby cakes? I was too busy thinking about how tasty dinner was.

Nova Scotia: Ocean of Love Mac & Cheese

From thought to pot to plate: 30 minutes

Serves: 2

Ingredients:

your favorite box of mac & cheese	1 tablespoon of butter
3 cloves of garlic, minced	1lb. of mussels in the shell
½ cup of fresh parsley, chopped	1/2 bottle of white wine
salt and pepper to taste	

Cook mac & cheese as directed on the box. Heat the butter in a frying pan. Add minced garlic, and then add the mussels, followed by the wine and cover with a lid until the shells open (about five minutes). Serve garnished with parsley on the side with mac & cheese. Mac-365 note: great first date meal.

Hustle those mussels people, to the ocean of love.

New Brunswick: Wicked Mac & Cheese

From thought to pot to plate: 30 minutes

Serves: 2

Ingredients:

your favorite box of mac & cheese	dash of olive oil
2 jalapenos, seeded and diced	½ cup of white onion, diced
1 chorizo sausage, sliced	salt and pepper to taste

Cook mac & cheese as directed on the box. Heat oil in a frying pan; add chorizo and sauté until cooked through, add onion, jalapeno, salt and pepper to taste; sauté for 2 minutes longer. Remove mixture from pan and place on mac and cheese.

Like I said, kick-it!

Newfoundland and Labrador: Kiss the Cod Mac & Cheese

From thought to pot to plate: 30 minutes
Serves: 2

Ingredients:

your favorite box of mac & cheese	1/2 lb. of cod cheeks
2 tablespoons of butter	salt and pepper to taste

Cook mac & cheese as directed on the box. Heat butter in the frying pan. Add cod cheeks and cook approximately 5 minutes; salt and pepper to taste. Toss in the mac & cheese.

Kiss the cod and don't get cheeky!

Prince Edward Island: Dive for a Pearl Mac & Cheese

From thought to pot to plate: 30 minutes
Serves: 2

Ingredients:

your favorite box of mac & cheese	1lb. of fresh PEI oysters
1 bottle of Tabasco sauce	1 bottle of horseradish
lots of lemon	shaved ice

Cook mac & cheese as directed on the box. Shuck oysters. Add a dash of Tabasco, horseradish and lemon... cool on shaved ice and suck back with mac & cheese chasers.

You want drama? Make things interesting and finish that bottle of Tabasco.

Northwest Territories: The Wreck of Yellowknife Mac & Cheese

From thought to pot to plate: 45 minutes

Serves: 2

Ingredients:

your favorite box of mac & cheese	dash of olive oil
1/2 pound of elk steak, cubed	salt and pepper to taste
dash of garlic pepper	1 tablespoon of BBQ sauce

Cook mac & cheese as directed on the box. Heat oil in mid-size skillet. Add the chopped elk and salt, pepper and garlic powder. Pour in your favorite BBQ sauce. Keep ingredients on burner until uniformly cooked to your liking and the meat is covered with BBQ sauce. Pour mixture from skillet and toss with mac & cheese.

Wrecked my car but we ate good!

Yukon: Dawson City Sour Toe Mac & Cheese

From thought to pot to plate: 45 minutes

Serves: 2

Ingredients:

your favorite box of mac & cheese	1/4 cup of butter
1/2 lb. of moose meat, cubed	1/4 cup of Jack Daniels
dash of cayenne pepper	dash of cream
salt and pepper to taste	1/4 cup of Parmesan cheese

Cook mac & cheese as directed on the box. Heat butter in the frying pan; add moose meat, cayenne pepper, salt and pepper. Whilst cooking to your liking, throw in the Jack Daniels and a dash of cream. Follow with a quarter cup of Parmesan cheese. Serve over mac & cheese.

Seriously? That was a toe?

Nunavut: On Ice Mac & Cheese

From thought to pot to plate: 15 minutes
Serves: 2

Ingredients:

your favorite box of mac & cheese	your favorite vodka
Nunavut ice	

Cook mac & cheese as directed on the box. While it's cooking, throw Nunavut ice (yes, that's right, from Nunavut – don't you have some handy?) in a glass and add vodka. Drink until the mac & cheese is cooked. Mix another one and serve.

Eat, drink and be mac happy!

Noodle Notes: ....

....

....

....

....

....

....

....

....

....

....

....

....

....

....

....

46

United States of Mac & Cheese

Alabama: Alabama Slammer Mac & Cheese

From thought to pot to plate: 40 minutes
Serves: 2

Ingredients:

your favorite box of mac & cheese	hot peppers, whole
1 egg, beaten	½ cup of flour (to cover the peppers)
dash of olive oil	salt and pepper to taste
1 peach, pitted and chopped	½ cup of red onion, diced
1 teaspoon of white vinegar	portion of cornbread

Cook mac & cheese as directed on the box. Beat egg, add a little water if needed. Dip hot peppers in the egg mix and then roll in the flour with salt and pepper. Heat oil and fry the peppers until golden brown. Combine the chopped peach, diced red onion and vinegar in separate bowl to make peach salsa. Serve whole battered peppers with side of peach salsa, cornbread and mac & cheese.

Yah, that was good… and friggin' spicy.

Alaska: Juno Salmon Mac & Cheese

From thought to pot to plate: 40 minutes
Serves: 2

Ingredients:

your favorite box of mac & cheese	2 medium sized fillets
1 tablespoon of olive oil	1 tablespoon of butter
juice of one lemon	salt and pepper to taste

Cook mac & cheese as directed on the box. Fry the salmon in the butter and oil mixture. Salt and pepper the fillets to taste. Cook approximately five minutes per side, depending on thickness. Squeeze lemon on the salmon and serve on the side with mac & cheese.

Juno how great this is?

Ohio: Chili Mac & Cheese

From thought to pot to plate: 30 minutes
Serves: 2

Ingredients:

your favorite box of mac & cheese	1 can of chili

Cook mac & cheese as directed on the box. Open can of chili. Heat and serve on the side of your mac & cheese.

Easy peasy mac & cheesy.

Arizona: Spiked Mac & Cheese

From thought to pot to plate: 40 minutes

Serves: 2

Ingredients:

your favorite box of mac & cheese	prepared piece of prickly pear cactus
dash of olive oil	juice of one lime
dash of cayenne pepper	salt and pepper to taste

Cook mac & cheese as directed on the box. Boil a midsize pot of water. Add cactus to the boiling water and cook for 10 minutes. Remove from the water and season with cayenne pepper and salt. Fry in the oil until lightly browned. Remove from the pan and squeeze lime on top. Serve with delicious mac & cheese.

Don't get prickly! Eat your mac!

Arkansas: Armadilla Thrilla Mac & Cheese

From thought to pot to plate: 30 minutes

Serves: 2

Ingredients:

your favorite box of mac & cheese	½ lb. of armadillo meat, cubed
2 ripe tomatoes, diced	1 cup of white onion, diced
2 cloves of garlic, minced	dash of seasoning salt
dash of olive oil	2 dill pickles, chopped

Cook mac & cheese as directed on the box. Heat oil and add armadillo meat, diced tomato, white onion, garlic and salt and pepper to taste. Cook for 10 to 15 minutes. Add to your mac & cheese. Here is the *thrilla*: chop two dill pickles and garnish the top of your meat.

Armadillo? Thanks! Don't mind if I do.

California: Health Club Mac & Cheese

From thought to pot to plate: 25 minutes
Serves: 2

Ingredients:

your favorite box of mac & cheese	generous handful of arugula
¼ small red onion, diced	½ tomato, diced
salt and pepper to taste	

Cook mac & cheese as directed on the box. Toss in the arugula, tomato and diced red onion on top of your cooked mac & cheese. Salt and pepper to taste.

Nice and light, gotta watch my hips - pass the aqua.

Colorado: Sunny Side Up Mac & Cheese

From thought to pot to plate: 40 minutes
Serves: 2

Ingredients:

your favorite box of mac & cheese	2 eggs
2 pieces of ham	2 pieces of processed cheese
dash of olive oil	

Put left over mac & cheese in a bowl. Stir in one egg. Shape noodles like two pieces of bread and fry in the oil for about 5 minutes each side. Remove and put aside. Warm ham and add a piece of cheese on top. Cook the other egg and duplicate the process. Lay a piece of the mac & cheese "bread" on top so it look like a sandwich.

Add ketchup, if you think it's a good idea...

Connecticut: Chuck Mac & Cheese

From thought to pot to plate: 30 minutes

Serves: 2

Ingredients:

your favorite box of mac & cheese	1lb of chuck steak, cubed
¼ cup of white onion, diced	1 green onion, sliced
½ cup of Cheddar cheese, grated	salt and pepper to taste
dash of olive oil	

Cook mac & cheese as directed on the box. Heat oil, add beef, and then add onion and green onion; continue to cook until vegetables are tender and beef is cooked through. Season with salt and pepper and plate with mac & cheese topped with Cheddar.

Enjoy!

Delaware: State Pride Chicken Mac & Cheese

From thought to pot to plate: 30 minutes

Serves: 2

Ingredients:

your favorite box of mac & cheese	2 chicken breasts, in bite-sized pieces
2 tablespoons of butter	dash of olive oil
salt and pepper to taste	½ an apple, diced

Cook mac & cheese as directed on the box. Salt and pepper the chicken and fry in a heated skillet with butter, olive oil and apple (approximately 4 minutes a side). Serve with mac and cheese.

This dish is also known as Blue Ribbon Mac & Cheese.

District of Columbia: Plantation Nation Mac & Cheese

From thought to pot to plate: 30 minutes
Serves: 2

Ingredients:

your favorite box of mac & cheese	1 plantain, in bite-sized pieces
dash of cayenne pepper	¼ cup olive oil
dash of salt	

Cook mac & cheese as directed on the box. Heat oil in frying pan. Once hot, add plantain and cook until brown. Remove from pan and rest on paper towel to take off excess oil. Put in a bowl, add cayenne and salt and toss in mac & cheese. Serve.

Enjoy!

Florida: Conked Out Mac & Cheese

From thought to pot to plate: 30 minutes
Serves: 2

Ingredients:

your favorite box of mac & cheese	1 lb. of conch meat, chopped
2 tablespoons of butter	2 tablespoons of olive oil
2 Scotch bonnet peppers, diced	cayenne pepper to taste
salt and pepper to taste	juice of 2 key limes

Cook mac & cheese as directed on the box. Heat butter and oil in frying pan; season conch with cayenne pepper, salt and pepper and sauté in the hot frying pan. Add the diced Scotch bonnets to the conch, sauté and add to the cooked mac & cheese with fresh lime juice.

Welcome to Florida, enjoy!

Georgia: Fly the Coup Mac & Cheese

From thought to pot to plate: 40 minutes

Serves: 2

Ingredients:

your favorite box of mac & cheese	1lb. of turkey wings
1 cup of flour	salt and pepper to taste
frying oil	2 Vidalia sweet onions, diced
1 peach, chopped	1 teaspoon white vinegar

Cook mac & cheese as directed on the box. Coat turkey wings in a flour, salt and pepper mixture. Deep-fry the wings in oil until cooked (approximately 20 minutes). Combine the peach, onion and vinegar to make salsa. Serve turkey with peach salsa and mac & cheese on the side.

Enjoy!

Hawaii: Hang Ten Mac & Cheese

From thought to pot to plate: 40 minutes

Serves: 2

Ingredients:

your favorite box of mac & cheese	1 can of processed ham
1 cup of mozzarella cheese, grated	frying oil
nori (edible seaweed), cut in triangles	salt and pepper to taste

Cook mac & cheese as directed on the box. Cut processed ham into ¼" strips and shape into surfboards. Fry shaped processed ham in oil until brown on both sides. Lay mac & cheese on bottom of the plate; form like a wave. Sprinkle the mozzarella cheese on top. Place your surfboards on top and garnish the wave with nori cut into triangles – those are the sharks!

Aloha ono!

Idaho: Potatoes Mac & Cheese Surprise

From thought to pot to plate: 60 minutes
Serves: 2

Ingredients:

your favorite box of mac & cheese	3 medium sized Idaho potatoes, sliced
2 white onions, sliced	1 cup of Cheddar cheese, grated
1 cup of milk	dash of olive oil
salt and pepper to taste	about a dozen regular potato chips

Preheat oven to 350°F. Cook mac & cheese as directed on the box. Layer sliced potatoes and onions in an oiled casserole dish. Sprinkle each layer with grated Cheddar. Pour a cup of milk on the top layer; add salt and pepper. Bake for 45 minutes. Once browned, add cooked mac & cheese and sprinkle crumbled potato chips on top.

Enjoy!

Wisconsin: "Cheese Head" Mac & Cheese

From thought to pot to plate: 20 minutes
Serves: 2

Ingredients:

your favorite box of mac & cheese	1 cup of your favorite cheese, grated
1 cob of Wisconsin corn	salt and pepper to taste

Cook mac & cheese as directed on the box. Once cooked, season and stir in cheese until melted. Serve with corn on the cob.

I've been called worse.

Illinois: Train Wreck Mac & Cheese

From thought to pot to plate: 30 minutes

Serves: 2

Ingredients:

your favorite box of mac & cheese	1/2 lb. fresh mushrooms, sliced
1 can of drained sauerkraut	3 slices of bacon, chopped
1 apple, chopped	salt and pepper to taste

Cook mac & cheese as directed on the box, *without adding the pouch of cheese.* Fry bacon. As bacon is cooking, add the mushrooms and apple. Once the bacon, mushrooms and apple are cooked, and the can of drained sauerkraut. Combine everything and sprinkle with the pouch of cheese. Add salt and pepper to taste. Add to the mac & cheese.

Enjoy!

Indiana: Gary Wants You Mac & Cheese

From thought to pot to plate: 40 minutes

Serves: 2

Ingredients:

your favorite box of mac & cheese	1lb. of pork tenderloin, cut in strips
1 green pepper, chopped	½ cup of white onion, diced
dash of olive oil	½ can of corn niblets, drained
salt and pepper to taste	

Cook mac & cheese as directed on the box. Sauté the green pepper and onion in olive oil; add the drained corn and salt and pepper to taste. Mix in with cooked mac & cheese.

Enjoy!

Iowa: Des Moines Mac & Cheese Salad

From thought to pot to plate: 60 minutes
Serves: 2

Ingredients:

your favorite box of mac & cheese	1 can of corn niblets, drained
2 sticks of celery, chopped	3 green onions, sliced
1 teaspoon of Dijon mustard	1/2 cup of mayonnaise
salt and pepper to taste	

Cook mac & cheese as directed on the box. Chill immediately once cooked. Combine the corn, green onions, celery, mayonnaise, mustard and salt and pepper. Add to the chilled mac & cheese.

Enjoy!

Kansas: Wild West BBQ Mac & Cheese

From thought to pot to plate: 40 minutes
Serves: 2

Ingredients:

your favorite box of mac & cheese	1lb. of venison steak
your favorite BBQ sauce	salt and pepper to taste

Cook mac & cheese as directed on the box. Season the steak with salt and pepper and brush with BBQ sauce. BBQ to your liking and let steak stand for five minutes after you take it off the grill. Cut into bite-sized pieces. Add the steak to mac & cheese.

Whoa! Slow down people!

Kentucky: Trouble Chicken Mac & Cheese

From thought to pot to plate: 35 minutes

Serves: 2

Ingredients:

your favorite box of mac & cheese	pre-made chicken fried steak
1/2 cup of cream	1 shot of bourbon
your favorite hot sauce	dash of olive oil
salt and pepper to taste	

Cook mac & cheese as directed on the box. Combine cream and bourbon into the mac & cheese and mix well. Fry chicken fried steak in oil. Lay chicken fried steak on a plate, top it off with the mac & cheese. Add your favorite hot sauce. Salt and pepper to taste.

Mint julep? Don't mind if I do…

Louisiana: Ragin' Cajun Mac & Cheese

From thought to pot to plate: 30 minutes

Serves: 2

Ingredients:

your favorite box of mac & cheese	1lb. of fresh crawfish, shelled
2 tablespoons of butter	3 green onions, sliced
dash of your favorite hot sauce	salt and pepper to taste
juice of one lemon	

Cook mac & cheese as directed on the box. Marinate the crawfish for 30 minutes in your favorite Cajun hot sauce and lemon juice. Sauté the crawfish in butter for approximately 5 minutes, until opaque. Add to the mac & cheese. Sprinkle chopped green onion on top. Salt and pepper to taste.

Enjoy!

Maine: Lux Lobster Mac & Cheese

From thought to pot to plate: 40 minutes
Serves: 2

Ingredients:

your favorite box of mac & cheese	1lb. of cooked Maine lobster meat
1/2 cup of cream	1/2 cup of Parmesan cheese
1/4 cup of butter	1 dash of nutmeg
salt and pepper to taste	

Cook mac & cheese as directed on the box. To make the sauce, heat cream, Parmesan cheese, butter and add nutmeg. Put cooked mac and cheese in a serving dish and add the warm lobster meat and the cream cheese sauce. Combine and serve. Salt and pepper to taste.

Impressed yet?

Maryland: Blue Crab Delight

From thought to pot to plate: 40 minutes
Serves: 2

Ingredients:

your favorite box of mac & cheese	1lb. of blue crab, in pieces
juice of one lemon	salt and pepper to taste

Cook mac & cheese as directed on the box. Boil water, add the blue crab and cook until your liking. Take out the crab and sit in ice water. Once chilled, remove the shell, take out the meat and put the crab on a serving dish and squeeze lemon on top and season to taste. Serve on the side with hot mac & cheese.

Keep chill with blue crab and hot with mac and cheese.

Massachusetts: Upside Down Mac & Cheese

From thought to pot to plate: 30 minutes

Serves: 2

Ingredients:

your favorite box of mac & cheese	1lb. of clams in the shell
1 cup of dry white wine	2 tablespoons of butter
3 cloves of garlic, minced	3 shallots, diced
juice of one lemon	¼ cup of fresh parsley, chopped
1 can of navy beans, baked	salt and pepper to taste

Cook mac & cheese as directed on the box. Melt butter in a large saucepan. Add minced garlic and shallots and sauté until soft. Rinse the clams and add to the saucepan, followed by the white wine. Cover and cook until the shells open. Remove from the heat and drain. Serve sprinkled with parsley and lemon juice atop your mac & cheese with a side of baked navy beans. Salt and pepper to taste.

Man that was tasty! I'm still trying to figure out the upside down part of it.

Noodle Notes: ....

....

....

....

....

....

....

....

....

....

....

....

....

Michigan: Takin' a Lickin' Mac & Cheese

From thought to pot to plate: 65 minutes
Serves: 2

Ingredients:

your favorite box of mac & cheese	1 beef tongue
1½ cup of Teriyaki sauce	1 can of beef broth
1 clove of garlic, minced	3 shallots, diced
salt and pepper to taste	

Preheat oven to 350°F. Cook mac & cheese as directed on the box. Place beef tongue in a baking dish. Add beef broth, teriyaki sauce, minced garlic and chopped shallots. Add salt and pepper to taste. Bake covered for one hour. Remove from pan and cut into bite-sized pieces. Mix in with mac & cheese.

Wow wee partner, I didn't expect the cow to talk back.

Minnesota: With the Soda Mac & Cheese

From thought to pot to plate: 35 minutes
Serves: 2

Ingredients:

your favorite box of mac & cheese	1lb. of trout fillets
½ package soda crackers, crushed	½ cup of flour
1 egg beaten, with a touch of water	2 tablespoons of butter
salt and pepper to taste	handful of morel mushrooms, sliced

Cook mac & cheese as directed on the box. Coat trout in flour; dip in the egg, then in the crushed soda crackers. Fry in the butter and oil (approximately 3 minutes per side). Add the morel mushrooms; salt and pepper to taste. Serve mac & cheese on the side.

Enjoy!

Mississippi: Mudflats Mac & Cheese

From thought to pot to plate: 40 minutes

Serves: 2

Ingredients:

your favorite box of mac & cheese	1lb. of catfish fillets
1 cup of flour	dash of Cajun spice
½ cup of frying oil	handful of parsley, chopped
salt and pepper to taste	

Cook mac & cheese as directed on the box. Coat catfish in flour, Cajun spice and salt and pepper; fry the catfish in oil (approximately 3-4 minutes depending on thickness). Serve the mac & cheese on the side and garnish with chopped parsley.

Get out the banjo and the bourbon!

Missouri: St. Louis Blues Mac & Cheese

From thought to pot to plate: 40 minutes

Serves: 2

Ingredients:

your favorite box of mac & cheese	1lb. of turkey gizzards
1 bottle of beer	½ cup of flour
2 tablespoon of oil	2 tablespoon of butter
½ cup of white onion, diced	2 cloves of garlic, minced
salt and pepper to taste	

Cook mac & cheese as directed on the box. Coat turkey gizzards in flour, salt and pepper. Fry mixture with garlic and onions for approximately 15-20 minutes, adding beer slowly. Mix in with the mac & cheese.

Enjoy!

Montana: Wagon Wheel Special Mac & Cheese

From thought to pot to plate: 30 minutes
Serves: 2

Ingredients:

your favorite box of mac & cheese	2 prairie oysters (bull calf testicles)
2 shallots, diced	2 cloves of garlic, minced
½ cup of flour	dash of olive oil
salt and pepper to taste	

Cook mac & cheese as directed on the box. Flatten the prairie oysters. Toss in flour and salt and pepper. Heat oil in frying pan, add shallots and garlic; sauté until soft. Add meat and cook approximately five minutes per side. Serve by plating mixture on top of mac & cheese.

For real? Bull balls?

Nebraska: Flap in the Wind Mac & cheese

From thought to pot to plate: 60 minutes
Serves: 2

Ingredients:

your favorite box of mac & cheese	1lb. of sweetbreads
4 shallots, diced	4 garlic cloves, minced
1 cup of white wine	salt and pepper to taste
1 corn on the cob, cooked	1 bag green salad

Preheat oven to 350°F. Cook mac & cheese as directed on the box. Put sweetbreads, shallots and garlic in a casserole dish and cover with the dry white wine. Add salt and pepper to taste. Cover and cook in the oven for 50 minutes. Serve the mac and cheese on the side with a green salad out of the bag and Nebraska corn on the cob.

You should know: this is not a dessert!

New Mexico: Jumpin' Beans Mac & Cheese

From thought to pot to plate: 30 minutes

Serves: 2

Ingredients:

your favorite box of mac & cheese	1 can of frijoles
2 green chiles, grilled, chopped	salt and pepper to taste

Cook mac & cheese as directed on the box. Combine green chiles with the mac & cheese. Salt and pepper to taste. Serve with a side of frijoles.

Enjoy!

Nevada: All-In Lucky Duck Mac & Cheese

From thought to pot to plate: 30 minutes

Serves: 2

Ingredients:

your favorite box of mac & cheese	1 BBQ duck, chopped
3 green onions, sliced	

Cook mac & cheese as directed on the box. Combine the duck with the mac and cheese, and garnish with green onion.

With this dish I would go all-in, too

New Hampshire: Live Free or Die Mac & Cheese

From thought to pot to plate: 30 minutes
Serves: 2

Ingredients:

your favorite box of mac & cheese	1 cup of pancetta, chopped
2 cups of frozen peas, thawed	½ small pumpkin squash, chopped
¼ cup frying oil	dash of maple syrup

Cook mac & cheese as directed on the box. Fry pancetta for approximately five minutes. Add pumpkin, followed by peas and a dash of maple syrup. Combine pancetta, pumpkin and peas with mac and cheese.

Making this dish will not be taxing.

New Jersey: Turn Pike Mac & Cheese

From thought to pot to plate: 60 minutes
Serves: 2

Ingredients:

your favorite box of mac & cheese	3/4 lb. pig cheeks, in bite-sized pieces
½ cup of white onion, diced	3 cloves of garlic, minced
1 can of stewed tomatoes	salt and pepper to taste

Preheat oven to 350°F. Cook mac & cheese as directed on the box. Place pig cheeks, onion, tomatoes and garlic in a casserole dish, then cover and cook for one hour. Remove from the oven after an hour and combine with mac and cheese.

Don't get all cheeky about this one.

New York: Dog City Mac & cheese

From thought to pot to plate: 40 minutes

Serves: 2

Ingredients:

your favorite box of mac & cheese	4 wieners
1 medium white onion, sliced	1 teaspoon of mustard
1 tablespoon of ketchup	4 hot dog buns
dash of olive oil	

Cook mac & cheese as directed on the box. Stir in the mustard and ketchup into the mac & cheese. Boil hot dogs until cooked. Fry the onion in oil until softened and golden brown. Toast the hot dog buns. Once toasted, lay the mac & cheese on each bun and then layer the hot dogs and cooked onion on top.

That's my style, batter up!

North Carolina: By the Sea Mac & Cheese

From thought to pot to plate: 35 minutes

Serves: 2

Ingredients:

your favorite box of mac & cheese	1 lb. of Atlantic blue marlin
1/4 cup of white dry wine	2 tablespoon of butter
dash of lemon pepper	salt to taste

Cook mac & cheese as directed on the box. Melt the butter in a frying pan. Season fish with lemon pepper and salt and place in pan. Sear the fish on both sides. Add ¼ cup of wine and flip occasionally until wine evaporates. Serve with mac & cheese on the side.

Enjoy!

North Dakota: Pleasant Pheasant Mac & Cheese

From thought to pot to plate: 35 minutes
Serves: 2

Ingredients:

your favorite box of mac & cheese	1lb. of pheasant meat, cubed
3 cloves of garlic, minced	½ cup of white onion, diced
dash of olive oil	salt and pepper to taste

Cook mac & cheese as directed on the box. Heat oil in a frying pan; sauté the garlic and onion until soft, then add the cubed pheasant and fry approximately 10 minutes, until cooked. Add salt and pepper to taste. Mix in the mac & cheese.

Enjoy!

Oklahoma: Bam Bam Mac & Cheese

From thought to pot to plate: 40 minutes
Serves: 2

Ingredients:

your favorite box of mac & cheese	1 cup of fresh okra, sliced
1 cup of cooked pork tenderloin, cubed	2 tablespoons of butter
½ cup of cream	1/3 cup black-eyed peas, drained
salt and pepper to taste	

Cook mac & cheese as directed on the box, *without adding the pouch of cheese.* In a saucepan, melt the butter and add the cream and contents of the cheese pouch. Add the okra and pork, followed by the cooked macaroni. Salt and pepper to taste. Serve with a side of black-eyed peas.

Enjoy!

Oregon: Ocean Spin Mac & Cheese

From thought to pot to plate: 30 minutes
Serves: 2

Ingredients:

your favorite box of mac & cheese	1lb. of shelled razor clams
2 tablespoons of butter	3 cloves of garlic, minced
dash of cayenne pepper	handful of Pacific Chanterelle mushrooms
1 teaspoon of horseradish	salt and pepper to taste

Cook mac & cheese as directed on the box. In a frying pan, melt the butter. Add the chopped garlic and mushrooms and sauté until soft. Rinse the clams and cook for about 7 minutes. Add cayenne pepper and horseradish. Serve with mac & cheese on the side.

If you want the spin, add a dash of creamed horseradish!

Pennsylvania: Philly Mac & Cheese

From thought to pot to plate: 40 minutes
Serves:

Ingredients:

your favorite box of mac & cheese	½ small white onion, sliced
1 green pepper, seeded and chopped	1 dash of olive oil
½ cup of fresh mushrooms, sliced	

Cook mac & cheese as directed on the box. In a heated frying pan, sauté the peppers, onions and mushrooms until soft. Serve mixture on top of your mac & cheese.

Enjoy!

Rhode Island: Road Kill Mac & Cheese

From thought to pot to plate: 30 minutes
Serves: 2

Ingredients:

your favorite box of mac & cheese	½ lb. of possum meat, cubed
1 green pepper, seeded and chopped	½ cup of white onion, diced
dash of olive oil	salt and pepper to taste

Cook mac & cheese as directed on the box. In a frying pan add oil and fry possum meat until brown. Add chopped green pepper and onion and fry another 10 minutes. Add salt & pepper and mix together with mac & cheese.

Awesome possum mac & cheese, or skunk, or raccoon...

South Carolina: Dilly Shrimp Mac & Cheese

From thought to pot to plate: 20 minutes
Serves: 2

Ingredients:

your favorite box of mac & cheese	2 tbsp. of fresh dill, chopped
1lb. of shrimp meat	1 tablespoon of capers
dash of olive oil	salt and pepper to taste
serving of collard greens	

Cook mac & cheese as directed on the box. In a heated pan, add oil and sauté shrimp until no longer opaque. Combine the dill, capers and salt and pepper and then mix in the mac & cheese, followed by the cooked shrimp. Serve with a side of collard greens.

Dillycious...

South Dakota: Hop 'n' Go Mac & Cheese

From thought to pot to plate: 35 minutes

Serves: 2

Ingredients:

your favorite box of mac & cheese	¾ lb. rabbit meat, cubed
½ cup of white onion, diced	3 cloves of garlic, minced
dash of your favorite hot sauce	dash of olive oil
salt and pepper to taste	

Cook mac & cheese as directed on the box. Sauté onion and garlic in oil until soft and add rabbit. Cook until done. Add hot sauce, salt and pepper. Combine with the mac & cheese.

Enjoy!

Tennessee: Slap Happy Mac & Cheese

From thought to pot to plate: 25 minutes

Serves: 2

Ingredients:

your favorite box of mac & cheese	1 can of sloppy Joe
1 jalapeno pepper, seeded and diced	1 tomato, diced
½ cup of cornmeal	salt and pepper to taste
dash of olive oil	1 egg, beaten

Cook mac & cheese as directed on the box. Heat the can of sloppy Joe in a saucepan and add diced tomato. Dip jalapeno whole into the egg and then coat with cornmeal. In a heated pan, cook coated jalapeno in olive oil. Place sloppy Joe on plate, with fried jalapeno on top; salt and pepper to taste. Serve with side of mac & cheese.

You can be slaphappy too if you eat this!

Virginia: Roll Over Mac & Cheese

From thought to pot to plate: 30 minutes
Serves: 2

Ingredients:

your favorite box of mac & cheese	1 ham steak, cubed
dash of olive oil	½ cup of frozen peas, thawed

Cook mac & cheese as directed on the box. Heat the oil in a frying pan. Quick fry the ham then add peas and combine with the mac & cheese.

Enjoy!

Texas: Alamo Mac & Cheese

From thought to pot to plate: 30 minutes
Serves: 2

Ingredients:

your favorite box of mac & cheese	½ lb. of rib eye steak, cubed
large handful of nacho chips	½ cup Tex-Mex cheese, grated
½ cup frozen corn, thawed	½ small sweet white onion, diced
1 cup green and red peppers, diced	1 tablespoon of chili powder
1 jalapeno pepper, diced	dash of olive oil

Cook mac & cheese as directed on the box. Fry cubed steak in a dash of olive oil; add onion, bell peppers, corn, jalapeno and chili powder. Once everything is cooked, top mac & cheese with the mixture and sprinkle cheese on top. Serve with handful of nacho chips.

That's one heck of a round up.

Federated States of Micronesia: Ella Bella Mac & Cheese

From thought to pot to plate: 20 minutes

Serves: 2

Ingredients:

your favorite box of mac & cheese	½ cup of fresh grated coconut
½ cup of Parmesan cheese, grated	salt and pepper to taste

Cook mac & cheese as directed on the box. Throw in grated coconut and Parmesan cheese, salt and pepper to taste. Combine and serve.

Enjoy!

Utah: Sweetheart Chicken Mac & Cheese

From thought to pot to plate: 30 minutes

Serves: 2

Ingredients:

your favorite box of mac & cheese	dash of Utah honey
½ lb. of chicken breast, cubed	1 small Spanish sweet onion, diced
2 cloves of garlic, minced	dash of cayenne pepper
dash of olive oil	1 tablespoon of white vinegar

Cook mac & cheese as directed on the box. Heat oil in a frying pan; add onion and garlic and sauté until soft. Add cubed chicken and cayenne pepper, followed by the vinegar. Drizzle finished chicken with honey. Serve on the side with mac & cheese.

Love this!

Vermont: Silent Sam Mac & Cheese

From thought to pot to plate: 40 minutes
Serves: 2

Ingredients:

your favorite box of mac & cheese	½ lb. of venison tenderloin, cubed
½ cup of white onion, diced	4 cloves of garlic, minced
½ cup of Silent Sam vodka	salt and pepper to taste
dash of olive oil	1 apple, sliced

Cook mac & cheese as directed on the box. Heat the oil in a frying pan; once hot add the chopped onion, minced garlic and chopped apple. Add cubed venison. Once the venison is cooked, add the vodka and simmer for 5 minutes. Salt and pepper to taste and place atop mac & cheese.

Enjoy!

Washington: Pacific Coast Highway Mac & Cheese

From thought to pot to plate: 40 minutes
Serves: 2

Ingredients:

your favorite box of mac & cheese	2 west coast salmon fillets
¼ cup of mayonnaise	2 small Walla Walla onions, diced
1 teaspoon of Dijon mustard	1 teaspoon of fresh dill, chopped
one lemon, cut in wedges	salt and pepper to taste

Preheat oven to 350°F. Cook mac & cheese as directed on the box. In a bowl, combine mayonnaise, mustard and dill; season with salt and pepper. Spread mayonnaise mixture on top of fillets and bake for 10-15 minutes in a covered pan. Serve with a squeeze of lemon with mac & cheese on the side.

Enjoy!

West Virginia: County Roads Mac & Cheese

From thought to pot to plate: 30 minutes

Serves: 2

Ingredients:

your favorite box of mac & cheese	1 trout fillet
juice of one lemon	1 tablespoon of butter
bunch of ramps, sliced	¼ cup of fresh parsley, chopped
salt and pepper to taste	

Cook mac & cheese as directed on the box. Heat butter in a frying pan; season trout with salt and pepper and cook in butter for approximately 3 minutes a side. Add ramps. Remove from the pan, sprinkle with parsley and lemon juice and serve with mac & cheese.

Enjoy!

Wyoming: Where the Buffalo Roam Mac & Cheese

From thought to pot to plate: 40 minutes

Serves: 2

Ingredients:

your favorite box of mac & cheese	1lb. of buffalo meat, ground
½ cup of white onion, diced	dash of seasoning salt
dash of cayenne pepper	frying oil

Cook mac & cheese as directed on the box. Fry ground bison meat and diced white onion in a frying pan until cooked. Add seasoning salt and cayenne pepper to taste. Combine the meat with the mac and cheese.

Let's go where the buffalo roam… right to my belly.

American Samoa: Macronesia & Cheese

From thought to pot to plate: 35 minutes
Serves: 2

Ingredients:

your favorite box of mac & cheese	½ lb. crayfish, cleaned
1 Thai red chili pepper, diced	3 cloves of garlic, minced
1 shallot, diced	1 teaspoon of fresh ginger, grated
dash of olive oil	salt and pepper to taste

Cook mac & cheese as directed on the box. Chop chili pepper, garlic, shallot and ginger. Heat oil in a frying pan; add crayfish and spices, salt and pepper. Once, cooked, toss with mac & cheese.

Hot enough for ya?

Guam: Curry in a Hurry Mac & Cheese

From thought to pot to plate: 30 minutes
Serves: 2

Ingredients:

your favorite box of mac & cheese	2 tablespoons of curry paste
½ can of garbanzo beans, drained	dash of olive oil
1 red pepper, diced	½ cup of red onion, diced
2 cloves of garlic, minced	2 rotis

Cook mac & cheese as directed on the box. Heat oil in a frying pan and sauté the onion, red pepper, curry paste and rinsed and drained garbanzo beans. Once soft, put mixture on top of the mac & cheese and serve with a side of roti.

Who is Roti and why is he in a hurry?

North Marianas: Phantom Mac & Cheese

From thought to pot to plate: 30 minutes

Serves: 2

Ingredients:

your favorite box of mac & cheese	½lb. bantam fowl, cubed
dash of chili pepper	dash of chili powder
dash of garlic powder	dash of olive oil
salt and pepper to taste	

Cook mac & cheese as directed on the box. Heat oil in a frying pan. Add cubed chicken and spices. Cook for 20 minutes or until done. Serve on top of your mac & cheese.

Enjoy!

Puerto Rico: Passion Mac & Cheese

From thought to pot to plate: 30 minutes

Serves: 2

Ingredients:

your favorite box of mac & cheese	1 cup of passion fruit, in bite-sized pieces
dash of cayenne pepper	

Cook mac & cheese as directed on the box. Set aside to cool. Prepare the fruit. Once the mac & cheese is cool, add the passion fruit and cayenne pepper and serve cold.

Enjoy!

Virgin Islands: On a Roll Mac & Cheese

From thought to pot to plate: 30 minutes

Serves: 2

Ingredients:

your favorite box of mac & cheese	bunch of callao, cleaned and cooked
dash of your favorite hot sauce	salt and pepper to taste
2 rotis	

Cook mac & cheese as directed on the box. Add cooked callao and season with hot sauce and salt and pepper. Serve mixture on top of heated roti with a side of mac & cheese.

Enjoy!

Noodle Notes: ....

....

....

....

....

....

....

....

....

....

....

....

....

....

....

Mac & Cheese in the Jolly Ole United Kingdom

Mac & Cheese Shepherds Pie

From thought to pot to plate: 45 minutes
Serves: 4

Ingredients:

2 boxes of your favorite mac & cheese	1½ lb. of lean ground beef
dash of olive oil	2 cups of frozen vegetables, thawed
2 cloves of garlic, minced	½ cup of white onion, diced
1 teaspoon of oregano	salt and pepper to taste
1 cup of Cheddar cheese, grated	1 small can of stewed tomatoes
1 tablespoon of ketchup	1 teaspoon of Worcestershire sauce

Preheat oven to 375°F. Cook mac & cheese as directed on the box. In a skillet heat a small amount of oil and brown the beef, onion and garlic until tender. Add tomatoes, veggies, Worcestershire, oregano, ketchup, salt and pepper, mix thoroughly and spread on bottom of casserole dish. Top with a layer of mac & cheese, then sprinkle Cheddar cheese on top. Bake for about 20 minutes or until bubbling and the top is golden brown.

"I say mate, that's fine Shepherd's Pie!"

Luke's Bangers & Mac

From thought to pot to plate: 45 minutes

Serves: 4

Ingredients:

box of mac & white Cheddar cheese	6 English-style sausages, cooked
2 tomatoes, sliced	1 cup of Cheddar cheese, grated
½ cup of breadcrumbs	1 teaspoon of melted butter
salt and pepper to taste	

Preheat oven to 350°F. Cook mac & cheese as directed on the box. Spread half of the prepared mac & cheese on the bottom of a greased casserole dish. Take three of the cooked sausages and split down the middle (butterfly). Place on top of the mac & cheese; top with a layer of sliced tomato and sprinkle with salt and pepper. Add ½ of the grated cheese. Repeat the mac & cheese, cooked sausage, tomato and cheese layers. Melt the butter into the breadcrumbs, then cover the top of the cheese with the buttered breadcrumbs. Bake for about 15 minutes or until bubbling and the top is golden brown. Let stand for 10 minutes before serving.

When is comes to bangers, no one bangs like my boy Luke! Enjoy!

Bubbles and Squeak Mac & Cheese

From thought to pot to plate: 25 minutes

Serves: 2

Ingredients:

your favorite box of mac & cheese	leftovers from Sunday roast
1 teaspoon of butter	salt and pepper to taste

Cook mac & cheese as directed on the box. Chop leftover meat, cabbage, potatoes, Brussels sprouts, peas and carrots… whatever you have. Combine and fry in a pan with butter. Serve with a side of mac & cheese, pickles and brown sauce.

Kenny says, "It's a fact! Mac & cheese with leftovers is better than steak and lobster."

Rolling Hills Mac & Cheese

From thought to pot to plate: 30 minutes

Serves: 3

Ingredients:

your favorite box of mac & cheese	1 bunch of fresh spinach
1 cup of green beans, in ½" pieces	½ cup of frozen peas, thawed
2 potatoes, sliced	1 cup of Cheddar cheese, grated
salt and pepper to taste	

Preheat oven to 350°F. Cook mac & cheese as directed on the box. Boil the potatoes until tender; add beans for the last minute of cooking time. Combine the mac & cheese, rinsed, destemmed and chopped spinach, green beans, potatoes and Cheddar in a casserole dish and bake for about 20 minutes or until bubbling and the top is golden brown. Let stand for 10 minutes before serving.

Top o' the day to you!

Noodle Notes: ....

....

....

....

....

....

....

....

....

....

....

....

....

Stone Cottage Mac & Cheese

From thought to pot to plate: 40 minutes
Serves: 2

Ingredients:

your favorite box of mac & cheese	1 teaspoon of butter, melted
1 cup of barley, cooked	½ cup of Guinness
2 teaspoons of fresh thyme, chopped	1 teaspoon of grainy mustard
salt and pepper to taste	1½ cups of breadcrumbs
2 cups of Cheddar cheese, grated	

Preheat oven to 350°F. Cook mac & cheese as directed on the box. Combine breadcrumbs, thyme, salt and pepper and melted butter; set aside. Transfer the pasta to a greased casserole dish and combine with the cheese, barley, mustard and Guinness. Top with the breadcrumb mixture and bake for about 20 minutes or until bubbling and the top is golden brown. Let stand for 10 minutes before serving.

Did you hear the one about the Irish doctor and his amazing round of golf?

Noodle Notes: ....

....

....

....

....

....

....

....

....

....

....

....

Mamma Mia Mac & Cheese

Mac & Cheese Skillet Cacciatore

From thought to pot to plate: 30 minutes
Serves:

Ingredients:

your favorite box of mac & cheese	4 chicken breasts, in bite-sized pieces
dash of olive oil	½ cup of white onion, diced
1½ teaspoons of Italian spice blend	1 can of stewed tomatoes
2 cups of chicken broth	1 cup of zucchini, chopped
2 teaspoons of Parmesan cheese, grated	

Cook mac & cheese as directed on the box *reserve the cheese packet.* Heat oil in large frying pan; cook chicken over medium-high heat. Add the cooked macaroni, chicken broth, onion, zucchini and Italian spice blend to the browned chicken. Stir to combine and bring to a boil. Reduce to a simmer, cover and cook for 3 minutes, stirring once or twice. Add tomatoes and reserved cheese powder; cook for another 3 or 4 minutes or until heated through. Top with Parmesan cheese and serve.

Enjoy!

MacAmore (a.k.a. Italian Flag Mac & Cheese)

From thought to pot to plate: 45 minutes

Serves: 6

Ingredients:

3 boxes of mac & white Cheddar cheese	½ cup of tomato sauce
½ teaspoon of garlic powder	1 teaspoon of Italian seasoning
¼ cup of pesto (Recipe Reference)	one drop of green food coloring
½ cup mozzarella cheese, grated	

Preheat oven to 350°F. Prepare mac & cheese as directed on the box, and keep the three portions separate. For the first batch add tomato sauce, garlic powder and Italian seasoning. For the second batch add pesto sauce and one drop of food coloring. In a 9" x 13" pan, arrange the mac & cheese to resemble the Italian flag, the first band is the pesto mac, the second band is the white Cheddar cheese and the third band is the tomato mac. Sprinkle the grated mozzarella cheese on the plain band and place in preheated oven until heated through and the cheese is melted.

Mac-365 note: Some say the colors of the Italian flag represent green for hope, white for faith and red for charity.

Noodle Notes:

Italian Chorizo Mac & Cheese Pie

From thought to pot to plate: 45 minutes

Serves: 2

Ingredients:

your favorite box of mac & cheese	4 Italian chorizo sausages
1 cup of fresh mushrooms, sliced	1 cup of white onion, diced
1 can of diced tomatoes	2 teaspoons of dried Italian seasoning
¼ teaspoon of red pepper flakes	1 cup of mozzarella cheese, grated
1 cup of breadcrumbs	salt and pepper to taste

Preheat oven to 350°F. Cook mac & cheese as directed on the box. Cook sausage (casings removed) in a large skillet until brown. Add the onion, garlic and red pepper flakes. Stir in tomatoes, tomato paste, Italian seasoning, salt and pepper to taste. Put the mac & cheese in the bottom of a greased casserole dish, then top with the sausage and tomato mixture. Cover with foil and bake for 25 minutes. Remove foil; sprinkle with breadcrumbs and mozzarella. Bake for another 10 minutes until bubbling and the top is golden brown. Let stand for 5 minutes before serving.

Enjoy!

Noodle Notes: ....

....

....

....

....

....

....

....

....

....

....

Mac & Cheese Bolognese

From thought to pot to plate: 45 minutes
Serves: 2

Ingredients:

your favorite box of mac & cheese	¼ cup of pancetta, chopped
1lb. of lean ground beef	1 cup of white onion, diced
2 carrots, peeled and diced	2 stalks of celery, chopped
3 cloves of garlic, minced	1 teaspoon of thyme
½ teaspoon of fennel seeds, crushed	1 teaspoon of dried oregano
1 teaspoon of red pepper flakes	1 cup of beef stock
1 cup of tomato paste	1 can of whole tomatoes, not drained
salt and pepper to taste	3 green onions, sliced
½ cup of Parmesan cheese, grated	½ cup of milk
¼ cup of fresh parsley, chopped	dash of olive oil

Cook mac & cheese as directed on the box. In skillet, fry pancetta until crispy; set aside to drain on paper towel. In same pan, heat oil and sauté onions, celery, and carrots until tender. Add garlic, green onions, fennel, thyme, oregano and red pepper flakes. Cook 2-3 minutes longer. Stir in broth and milk; season with salt and pepper. Cook over medium to low heat for about 10 minutes. Add tomato paste, whole tomatoes and milk. Turn heat to low and simmer for 12 minutes more. Add reserved pancetta. Serve on a bed of mac and cheese. Garnish with parsley and Parmesan.

Mamma mia!

Mac & Cheese Lasagna

From thought to pot to plate: 45 minutes
Serves: 2

Ingredients:

your favorite box of mac & cheese	1lb. of ground Italian sausage
1 cup of fresh mushrooms, sliced	½ cup of carrots, shredded
1¼ cups of tomato sauce	½ cup of green pepper, diced
¼ cups of mozzarella cheese, grated	¼ cup Parmesan cheese, grated

Preheat oven to 350°F. Cook mac & cheese as directed on the box. In skillet over medium heat, brown sausage and drain, then add mushrooms, carrots and green pepper, Sauté for 4-5 minutes and add tomato sauce and stir to combine. In a greased casserole dish, put in half the mac & cheese on the bottom, then top with half the meat and half the cheese, and repeat the process. Bake for about 25 minutes or until bubbling and the top is golden brown. Let stand for 10 minutes before serving.

Enjoy!

Noodle Notes: ....
....
....
....
....
....
....
....
....
....
....
....
....

Chicken Parmesan Mac & Cheese

From thought to pot to plate: 45 minutes
Serves: 4

Ingredients:

your favorite box of mac & cheese	4 chicken breasts, pounded to ½" thick
2 eggs, beaten	½ cup of milk
2 tablespoons olive oil	1 cup of breadcrumbs
1½ cup of mozzarella cheese, grated	2 jars of tomato sauce
1 cup of Parmesan cheese, grated	

Preheat oven to 350°F. Cook mac & cheese as directed on the box. In a bowl, whisk together the egg and milk. Dip the chicken breasts in the milk and egg mixture, and then in the breadcrumbs. Heat the olive oil in a skillet on medium high heat and cook the chicken in the hot oil until golden brown – about 5 minutes per side. Set chicken in a greased casserole dish; sprinkle with mozzarella and pour tomato sauce on top, then finish with Parmesan cheese. Bake for about 15 minutes or until bubbling and the top is golden brown. Serve on bed of mac & cheese.

Enjoy!

Noodle Notes: ....
....
....
....
....
....
....
....
....
....

On Top of Old Macky... All Covered With Cheese

From thought to pot to plate: 60 minutes

Serves: 4

Ingredients:

your favorite box of mac & cheese	1lb. of lean ground beef
¼ cup of sour cream	1½ cup of mozzarella cheese, grated
½ cup of breadcrumbs	1 egg, beaten
½ cup of white onion, chopped	2 cloves of garlic, minced
½ cup of club soda	½ cup of Parmesan, grated
2 tablespoons of parsley, chopped	salt and pepper to taste
dash of olive oil	

Preheat oven to 350°F. Prepare meatballs using the ground beef, garlic and beat in club soda a little at a time, followed by the egg, salt and pepper. Add breadcrumbs, cheese and parsley. Chill mixture for half an hour, then roll into medium sized meatballs. Cook the meatballs in olive oil in a frying pan over medium to high heat until browned on all sides and then lower the heat to cook through; approximately for 15 minutes. Remove from pan once cooked and drain on a paper towel. Cook mac & cheese as directed on the box, add 1 cup of mozzarella cheese and sour cream and mix well. Spoon mac mixture into 9"x 9" greased casserole dish, top with meatballs and remaining mozzarella and Parmesan cheese, and bake for about 15 minutes or until bubbling and the top is golden brown.

"On top of macky, all covered with cheese, I lost my poor meatball, when somebody sneezed..." Don't let this happen to you! Stay vigilant and ready to protect your macky!

Mac & Cheese Primavera

From thought to pot to plate: 35 minutes

Serves: 2

Ingredients:

your favorite box of mac & cheese	dash of olive oil
2 tablespoons of butter	4 green onions, sliced
2 cloves of garlic, minced	1 small zucchini, thinly sliced
1½ cups of broccoli florets	2 large tomatoes, diced
12 sugar snap peas	1 cup of mushrooms, sliced
½ cup of parsley, finely chopped	1 tablespoon of grainy mustard
salt and pepper to taste	½ cup of vegetable broth
¼ cup of Parmesan cheese, grated	salt and pepper to taste

Cook mac & cheese as directed on the box. In skillet heat olive oil and butter over medium-high heat and add the vegetables, mustard, salt and pepper. Cover and cook for five minutes or until vegetables are tender. Stir in vegetable broth and heat through. Serve on a bed of mac & cheese, garnished with Parmesan.

Enjoy!

Baked Caprese Mac & Cheese

From thought to pot to plate: 40 minutes
Serves: 4

Ingredients:

your favorite box of mac & cheese	1 pint of Campari tomatoes, quartered
2 cloves of garlic, minced	½ cup of red onion, diced
1 tablespoon of olive oil	juice of one lemon
salt and pepper to taste	½ cup of fresh basil, chopped
drizzle of balsamic vinegar reduction	2 cups of bocconcini cheese, sliced

Preheat oven to 350°F. In a baking dish, combine tomatoes, garlic, onion, olive oil, lemon juice, salt and pepper. Toss to coat and bake for 10 minutes. Remove and set aside. Cook mac & cheese as directed on the box. Fold the bocconcini, basil and tomato mixture into the mac & cheese and bake in a greased casserole dish for 15 minutes or until heated through. Serve drizzled with balsamic vinegar reduction.

Mamma mia!

Noodle Notes: ....
....
....
....
....
....
....
....
....
....
....
....

Pancetta Mac & Fromaggio

From thought to pot to plate: 45 minutes
Serves: 2

Ingredients:

your favorite box of mac & cheese	1 cup of pancetta, chopped
1 tablespoon of balsamic vinegar	1 teaspoon of fresh rosemary, chopped
½ cup of red onion, diced	2 cloves of garlic, minced
½ cup of Fontina cheese, grated	1 tablespoon of Parmesan cheese
salt and pepper to taste	

Preheat oven to 350°F. Cook mac & cheese as directed on the box. In a large skillet cook the pancetta until crispy, remove from heat and set on paper towel to drain. Add the onion, garlic and balsamic vinegar to the skillet and cook until caramelized. Combine the mac & cheese, balsamic onions, rosemary, salt, pepper and pancetta in a casserole dish and top with grated Fontina and Parmesan cheese. Bake for about 20 minutes or until bubbling and the top is golden brown. Let stand for 10 minutes before serving.

Deliziosissima!

Noodle Notes:

....

....

....

....

....

....

....

....

....

Mac & Cheese alla Carbonara

From thought to pot to plate: 30 minutes
Serves: 2

Ingredients:

your favorite box of mac & cheese	2 cloves of garlic, minced
½ cup of red onion, diced	6 slices of bacon, chopped
1 egg yolk	1 egg, beaten
1 tablespoon of dried marjoram	1 tablespoon of butter
3 tablespoons of breadcrumbs	½ cup of Parmesan cheese, grated
¼ cup of parsley, chopped	salt and pepper to taste

Cook mac & cheese as directed on the box. In a skillet, cook the chopped bacon until crispy. Sauté the garlic and onion until soft; add two tablespoons of breadcrumbs, salt and pepper to the mixture. Beat the egg and egg yolk in a separate bowl, along with the marjoram and grated Parmesan, and fold into the mac & cheese, along with butter. Serve sprinkled with the remaining breadcrumbs and parsley.

Noodle Notes: ....

....

....

....

....

....

....

....

....

....

....

....

Chicken Marbella Mac & Cheese

From thought to pot to plate: 45 minutes
Serves: 4

Ingredients:

your favorite box of mac & cheese	4 chicken breasts, in bite-sized pieces
1 cup of green olives, pitted	1 tablespoon of capers, drained
½ cup of red wine vinegar	2 cloves of garlic, minced
5 bay leaves	1 teaspoon of dry oregano
1 tablespoon of olive oil	6 plums, pitted
salt and pepper to taste	1 cup of brown sugar
1 cup of white wine	½ cup of parsley, chopped

Combine the chicken, capers, garlic, olives, bay leaves, red wine vinegar, oregano, olive oil, salt, pepper and parsley in a large bowl or zip top plastic bag. Marinate in the refrigerator for eight hours, turning occasionally. Preheat oven to 350°F. Cook mac & cheese as directed on the box. Arrange the chicken in a single layer in a greased casserole dish; then pour marinade evenly over chicken, followed by brown sugar and wine. Bake for about 40 minutes, basting frequently. Serve on a bed of mac & cheese.

Enjoy!

Tetrazzini Mac & Cheese

From thought to pot to plate: 30 minutes
Serves: 4

Ingredients:

your favorite box of mac & cheese	4 chicken breasts, in bite-sized pieces
2 cups of fresh mushrooms, sliced	1 red pepper, chopped
1 cup of white onion, minced	4 cloves of garlic, minced
½ cup of cream cheese	¼ cup of flour
¼ cup of Parmesan cheese, grated	1/8 teaspoon of nutmeg
1 cup of chicken broth	½ cup of mozzarella cheese, grated
salt and pepper to taste	1 tablespoon of thyme
1 cup of frozen peas, thawed	dash of olive oil
1 cup of breadcrumbs	

Preheat oven to 350°F. Cook mac & cheese as directed on the box. In a skillet cook the chicken and mushrooms, garlic, onion, peas and red pepper on medium heat. Remove from heat and set aside. Add the cream cheese, nutmeg, thyme and broth to the skillet and bring to a boil, whisk in flour, stirring constantly. In a greased casserole dish, combine the mac & cheese, chicken and cream cheese mixture. Top with breadcrumbs and mozzarella and bake for about 30 minutes or until bubbling and the top is golden brown.

Enjoy!

Chicken Piccata Mac & Cheese

From thought to pot to plate: 40 minutes
Serves: 4

Ingredients:

your favorite box of mac & cheese	4 chicken breasts
½ cup of red onion, diced	1 teaspoon of capers
1 cup of chicken broth	2 tablespoons of flour
salt and pepper to taste	2 teaspoons of olive oil
2 teaspoons of lemon zest	2 tablespoons of lemon juice
2 cloves of garlic, minced	1 teaspoon of dry mustard
3 green onions, chopped	

Cook mac & cheese as directed on the box. Place each chicken breast in a plastic bag and lightly pound to reduce the thickness; remove from bag. In a shallow dish combine flour, salt and pepper and coat each chicken breast with the mixture. Cook coated chicken breasts in a large skillet until browned evenly. Add broth, lemon zest and juice, garlic, dry mustard, red onion, capers and a pinch of salt. Bring mixture to a boil and reduce heat to simmer. Add the green onions and cook for another two minutes. Serve cooked chicken on a bed of mac & cheese and drizzle cooking liquid on top.

Enjoy!

Mac & Cheese Bologna Bowls

From thought to pot to plate: 30 minutes
Serves: 3

Ingredients:

your favorite box of mac & cheese	dash of olive oil
12 slices of bologna	1 cup of Cheddar cheese, grated
1½ cups of breadcrumbs	2 teaspoons of dried Italian seasoning
4 tablespoons of butter	2 teaspoons of garlic oil

Cook mac & cheese as directed on the box. Heat olive oil in a skillet and fry bologna slices until curled or bubbled in the centre, forming a "bowl" shape. Fill the bologna bowls with mac & cheese, top with Cheddar cheese and place on a sheet pan. In a separate bowl, combine the breadcrumbs, Italian seasoning and butter. Top the mac & cheese bologna bowls with the breadcrumb mixture and heat under broiler until crumbs are golden brown.

Enjoy!

Noodle Notes: ....
....
....
....
....
....
....
....
....
....
....
....
....

Mac & Cheese Chorizo Lasagna

From thought to pot to plate: 45 minutes
Serves: 4

Ingredients:

your favorite box of mac & cheese	1lb. of ground Italian sausage
1 jar of roasted garlic tomato sauce	1½ cups of mozzarella, grated
½ cup of breadcrumbs	

Preheat oven to 350°F. Cook mac & cheese as directed on the box. Brown the sausage, casings removed, in a heated skillet and place on paper towel to drain. In a greased casserole dish, place the mac & cheese on the bottom, add ground sausage layer, tomato sauce layer and top with cheese and breadcrumbs. Bake for about 15 minutes or until bubbling and the top is golden brown. Let stand for 10 minutes before serving.

Enjoy!

Mac & Cheese Florentine

From thought to pot to plate: 35 minutes
Serves: 4

Ingredients:

your favorite box of mac & cheese	dash of olive oil
2 cloves of garlic, minced	salt and pepper to taste
½ cup of fresh mushrooms, sliced	pinch of nutmeg
1 bunch of fresh spinach	1 cup of Parmesan cheese, grated

Cook mac & cheese as directed on the box. Heat olive oil in a large pan over medium heat and add garlic, mushrooms, pepper, salt and nutmeg, followed by the stemmed spinach and sauté for about a minute until spinach is wilted. Add mac & cheese to the pan and stir to combine. Top with Parmesan and heat through till cheese is melted.

Molto gusto!

Mac & Cheese Takes Europe

Coq au Vin Mac & Cheese

From thought to pot to plate: 45 minutes

Serves: 4

Ingredients:

your favorite box of mac & cheese	1 cup of pancetta, chopped
1½ cups of white onion, diced	8 chicken thighs (with skin and bone)
3 cloves of garlic, minced	2 tablespoons of cognac
2 cups of red wine	1 cup of chicken stock
1 teaspoon of tomato paste	2 cups of button mushrooms, sliced
2 teaspoons of fresh thyme, chopped	1 tablespoon of fresh parsley, chopped
½ cup of scallions, chopped	2 tablespoons of flour
3 tablespoons of butter	salt and pepper to taste

In a large stockpot, fry the pancetta over medium heat and then transfer with a slotted spoon to paper towel to drain. Generously salt and pepper the chicken and place in the pot, skin side down. Cook each side for about 7 minutes. Transfer the chicken to the plate with the pancetta. Remove all but about one tablespoon of fat from the pan and set aside. Add the onion and garlic into the pot, then add the cognac and deglaze the pan. Allow most of the liquid to evaporate, then add red wine, chicken stock and tomato paste and combine. Return the chicken and pancetta to the pot and cover with liquid. Partially cover the pot and simmer on medium low heat for about 30 minutes. Add the flour to the reserved fat and combine. When the chicken is cooked, transfer to a plate and cover. Add the mushrooms to the pot on medium heat and simmer uncovered for about 15 minutes. Add a few tablespoons of the sauce to the fat/flour paste and stir; add this to the sauce in the pan one spoonful at a time to blend. Add the chicken and pancetta to the pot to reheat and coat with sauce. Serve garnished with parsley on a bed of mac & cheese.

Oh là là! C'est formidable!

Savory Mac & Cheese Crepes

From thought to pot to plate: 45 minutes
Serves: 2

Ingredients:

box of mac & white Cheddar cheese	your favorite crepe batter
2 tablespoons of olive oil	1 large white onion, thinly sliced
½ cup of dry white wine	1 teaspoon of sugar

Cook mac & cheese as directed on the box. Prepare the crepe batter and cook. Stack the cooked crepes on a plate with wax paper in between each one and keep warm in a low temperature oven. In a heated skillet sauté the onion in olive oil until soft. Add white wine and reduce, then add the sugar to caramelize the onion. Place crepe on plate and place some mac & cheese down the centre, top with desired amount of onion, fold one side of the crepe over filling to cover, and then the other side over the first.

Bon appétit!

Noodle Notes: ....

....

....

....

....

....

....

....

....

....

....

....

Spanish Mac & Cheese Casserole

From thought to pot to plate: 45 minutes

Serves: 2

Ingredients:

your favorite box and mac & cheese	1 tablespoon of olive oil
1lb. of lean ground beef	½ cup of white onion, diced
1 cup fresh mushrooms, sliced	1 clove of garlic, minced
1 can of sliced black olives, drained	1 can of chopped green chiles
1 can of tomato soup	1 can of corn niblets, drained
1 teaspoon of chili powder	½ cup of mozzarella cheese, grated
salt and pepper to taste	

Preheat oven to 350°F. Cook mac & cheese as directed on box. Brown meat in oil; add onion, mushrooms and garlic and cook until soft. Remove from heat and stir in olives, chilies, tomato soup, corn and seasonings. Top with grated mozzarella. Place in greased casserole dish and bake for about 15 minutes or until bubbling and the top is golden brown. Let stand for 10 minutes before serving.

Enjoy!

Noodle Notes: ....
....
....
....
....
....
....
....
....
....

Mac & Blue Cheese Bomb

From thought to pot to plate: 35 minutes

Serves: 2

Ingredients:

your favorite box of mac & cheese	6 slices of prosciutto, chopped
1 tablespoon of butter	2 medium shallots, diced
3 cloves of garlic, minced	¼ cup of flour
2½ cups whole milk	1/2 cup of blue cheese, crumbled
salt and pepper to taste	1 cup of panko breadcrumbs
½ cup of parsley, chopped	½ cup of white Cheddar cheese, grated

Preheat oven to 350°F. Cook mac & cheese as directed on the box. In a large skillet, melt the butter and add the shallots and garlic, sautéing until soft. Fold in the flour and cook for a minute longer. Gradually whisk in the milk. Reduce to a low heat and add the blue cheese followed by the parsley. Simmer until the mixture thickens slightly and add salt and pepper to taste. Fold the mixture into the mac & cheese and transfer to a greased casserole dish. Put the prosciutto in the skillet and cook until crispy; about a minute - and add to the casserole. Sprinkle the top with panko and Cheddar. Bake for about 15 minutes or until bubbling and the top is golden brown. Let stand for 10 minutes before serving.

See? Da bomb!

Mac & Cheese Seafood Pancetta Paella

From thought to pot to plate: 45 minutes

Serves: 2

Ingredients:

your favorite box of mac & cheese	dash of olive oil
7 slices of pancetta, chopped	¼ teaspoon of saffron
3 cloves of garlic, minced	½ cup of fresh parsley, chopped
1 cup of white onion, diced	2 cups of chicken stock
1 teaspoon of paprika	1 cup of frozen peas, thawed
12 prawns, peeled and deveined	½ lb. of mussels in the shell
1 can of stewed tomatoes	1 red pepper, chopped
salt and pepper to taste	

Cook mac & cheese as directed on the box. Cook chopped pancetta until crispy. Set aside on a paper towel to drain. Sauté the onion and garlic in the pan until soft, and add the paprika and chicken stock. Simmer on medium heat for about 7 minutes, and then add the saffron, stewed tomatoes, red pepper, peas, prawns and mussels. Simmer on low for about 30 minutes until the liquid has dissolved. Serve on a bed of mac & cheese.

Pretty fancy, eh?

Shainey's Mac & Cheese Cordon Bleu

From thought to pot to plate: 45 minutes
Serves: 4

Ingredients:

your favorite box of mac & cheese	4 chicken breasts
salt and pepper to taste	6 slices of Swiss cheese
4 slices of Black Forest ham	½ cup of seasoned breadcrumbs
¼ cup of flour	dash of paprika

Preheat oven to 350°F. Cook mac & cheese as directed on the box. Pound chicken breasts to ¼" thickness and coat each piece of chicken on both sides with a combination of flour, paprika, salt and pepper. Place one cheese slice and one ham slice on top of each breast. Roll each breast and secure with a toothpick. Place in a greased sheet pan and sprinkle evenly with breadcrumbs. Bake chicken for 30 minutes, or until no longer pink. Remove from oven, and place ½ a cheese slice on top of each breast. Return to oven for 3 minutes, or until cheese has melted. Remove toothpicks and serve immediately with a side of mac & cheese.

When our girl Shainey cooks Mac & Cheese Cordon Bleu, there is nothing bleu about it - it's dang delicious, like the way she looks! Enjoy!

Noodle Notes: ....

....

....

....

....

....

....

....

....

....

Danny's Baked Mac & Cheese Pie

From thought to pot to plate: 50 minutes

Serves: 2

Ingredients:

your favorite box of mac & cheese	dash of olive oil
1lb. of lean ground beef	1 tube of frozen crescent rolls
½lb. of fresh mushrooms, sliced	2 cups of frozen vegetables, thawed
½ cup of water	1 can of cream of mushroom soup
1 cup of white onion, diced	4 slices of processed cheese
salt and pepper to taste	

Preheat oven to 375°F. Cook mac & cheese as directed on the box. In a large oven-proof skillet cook the ground beef and add the mushrooms and onion on medium heat for approximately 10 minutes. Stir in the rest of the vegetables, soup, water, salt and pepper, bringing the mixture to a boil – then add the cheese and stir well. Remove the skillet from the stove. Unroll the dough triangles and place on top of beef and vegetable mixture, covering the top and place skillet in the oven. Bake for about 20 minutes until the top is golden brown. Remove from the oven and let stand for 10 minutes before serving.

Danny says, "Don't tell your friends about this so you can have it all to yourself – they can stay home and cook their own dinner!"

Creamy Chicken Mac & Cheese Bake

From thought to pot to plate: 40 minutes

Serves: 4

Ingredients:

2 boxes of your favorite mac & cheese	4 chicken breasts, in bite-sized pieces
3 cups of broccoli florets	4 slices of bacon, chopped
½ cup of chicken broth	½ cup of cream cheese
¾ cup Mozzarella cheese, grated	2 tablespoons of Parmesan cheese

Preheat oven to 375°F. Cook the pasta as directed on the box, adding the broccoli florets for the last 3 minutes, and then drain together. Cook the bacon until crispy, then set aside on paper towel to drain. Cook the chicken for 5 minutes or until no longer pink, stirring frequently, and then stir in broth; simmer for approximately 3 minutes or until chicken is cooked. Add cream cheese; cook and stir on low heat until cheese is melted, then stir in ½ cup of mozzarella. Add the pasta, bacon and the broccoli to the chicken mixture, mixing lightly. Spoon mixture into greased casserole dish and cover. Bake for about 15 minutes, then remove foil and sprinkle on Parmesan and bake for another 5 minutes or until bubbling and the top is golden brown. Let stand for 10 minutes before serving.

Enjoy!

Noodle Notes: ....

....

....

....

....

....

....

....

Mac & Cheese Chicken Casserole

From thought to pot to plate: 45 minutes
Serves: 2

Ingredients:

your favorite box of mac & cheese	1lb. of ground chicken
dash of olive oil	½ cup of white onion, diced
1 cup of frozen vegetables, thawed	1 can of cream of chicken soup
1 teaspoon of thyme	salt and pepper to taste
1 cup of breadcrumbs	

Preheat oven to 350°F. Cook mac & cheese as directed on the box. In a frying pan, brown the chicken and onion in oil. Add the frozen mixed vegetables, soup, thyme and salt and pepper to taste. Combine ingredients with the mac & cheese and transfer everything to a greased casserole dish. Cover with breadcrumbs. Bake for about 15 minutes or until bubbling and the top is golden brown. Let stand for 10 minutes before serving.

Enjoy!

Noodle Notes: ....

....

....

....

....

....

....

....

....

....

....

Margaret's Chicken Broccoli Mac & Cheese

From thought to pot to plate: 45 minutes
Serves: 4

Ingredients:

2 boxes of your favorite mac & cheese	1 cup of broccoli florets
3 chicken breasts, in bite-sized pieces	½ cup of chicken broth
½ cup of cream cheese	1 cup of mozzarella, grated
2 tablespoons of Parmesan cheese	dash of olive oil

Preheat oven to 375°F. Cook the macaroni as directed on the box. Add the broccoli for the last two minutes, and then drain together. Heat olive oil a large skillet on medium high heat. Add the chicken and cook for five minutes; then stir in broth and simmer for three minutes until the chicken is cooked. Add cream cheese and stir on low heat until cheese is blended in, then stir in ½ cup of mozzarella. Add the pasta and broccoli to the chicken mixture and combine; spoon into a greased casserole dish and cover. Bake for 15 minutes or until heated through. Remove cover and sprinkle the Parmesan and the rest of the mozzarella and bake until bubbling and golden brown. Let stand for 10 minutes before serving.

I dedicate this delicious dish to my friends: Noodle, Mom and Margaret - who is also a dish. Enjoy!

Noodle Notes: ....

....

....

....

....

....

....

....

....

There is a Heaven Mac & Cheese

From thought to pot to plate: 60 minutes
Serves: 4

Ingredients:

your favorite box of mac & cheese	4 baking potatoes
2 tablespoon of olive oil	1 cup of Tex-Mex cheese, grated
4 slices of bacon, chopped	¼ cup sour cream
2 green onions, sliced	1 clove of garlic, minced

Preheat oven to 400°F. Bake the potatoes in the oven for approximately 40 minutes and remove from the oven, turning the temperature down to 350°F. Cook mac & cheese as directed on the box. Cook the bacon until crispy and set aside on a paper towel to drain. Halve cooked potatoes lengthwise, scoop out the centres – leaving ¼" thick shells. Put the excess potato in the fridge for tomorrow's hash browns. Place potato skins on a sheet pan and brush interiors with oil and minced garlic. Spoon the mac & cheese into the potato skins, top with cheese and bake for about 10 minutes or until bubbling and the top is golden brown. Top with bacon, sour cream and green onion and serve as a side dish.

Enjoy!

Noodle Notes: ....
....
....
....
....
....
....
....
....
....
....

I'll Be Bock Mac & Cheese

From thought to pot to plate: 45 minutes
Serves: 2

Ingredients:

your favorite box of mac & cheese	2 slices of bacon, chopped
½ cup of white onion, diced	salt and pepper to taste
½ teaspoon of dried mustard	½ teaspoon of cayenne
¼ cup of flour	½ cup of amber beer
1 tablespoon of cream cheese	1 cup of panko breadcrumbs
½ cup of Cheddar cheese, grated	½ cup of Parmesan cheese, grated

Preheat oven to 350°F. Cook mac & cheese as directed on the box. In a skillet cook bacon until crispy; then set aside on a paper towel to drain. In the same skillet, cook the onion until soft and add the salt, pepper, mustard powder and cayenne pepper. Whisk in the flour until smooth, then add the beer and cream cheese and cook until mixture is blended. Combine the mac & cheese, bacon, seasoned beer mixture and the Cheddar in a greased casserole dish and top with Parmesan and panko. Bake for about 25 minutes or until bubbling and the top is golden brown. Let stand for 10 minutes before serving.

Enjoy!

Mac & Cheese with Anchovies and Garlic

From thought to pot to plate: 35 minutes

Serves: 2

Ingredients:

your favorite box of mac & cheese	2 cloves of garlic, minced
1 cup of panko breadcrumbs	2 teaspoons of butter
2oz. of anchovy fillets, finely chopped	juice of two lemons
4 green onions, sliced	¼ cup of olive oil

Cook mac & cheese as directed on the box. Melt butter in frying pan; add garlic and panko crumbs and stir until golden brown. Put mac & cheese in a large bowl with the rest of the ingredients and toss gently to combine. Serve.

Enjoy!

Mac & Cheese with Clam Sauce

From thought to pot to plate: 35 minutes

Serves: 2

Ingredients:

box of white Cheddar mac & cheese	1 tablespoon of olive oil
2 cloves of garlic, minced	½ cup of white onion, diced
1 can of baby clams, including liquid	¼ cup of fresh parsley, chopped
salt and pepper to taste	

Cook mac & cheese as directed on the box. Heat oil in a frying pan, add garlic and onions and cook until soft; add the clams and liquid, stir to combine. Simmer until liquid reduced by half and then add fresh parsley. Add mac & cheese to the mixture and heat through.

Enjoy!

Mac & Cheese with Ham and Spinach

From thought to pot to plate: 35 minutes
Serves: 2

Ingredients:

your favorite box of mac & cheese	1 ham steak, fried and cubed
1 cup of fresh spinach	1 teaspoon of garlic salt
1 teaspoon of fresh cracked black pepper	½ cup mozzarella cheese, grated
1 tablespoon of melted butter	½ cup fresh breadcrumbs

Preheat oven to 375°F. Cook mac & cheese as directed on the box. Rinse, stem and chop the spinach. Stir in ham, spinach, garlic salt, pepper and mozzarella cheese. Transfer mixture to a greased casserole dish. Toss breadcrumbs with melted butter and sprinkle over pasta. Bake for about 15 minutes or until bubbling and the top is golden brown.

Enjoy!

Mac & Cheese Stuffed Potatoes

From thought to pot to plate: 45 minutes
Serves: 6

Ingredients:

your favorite mac & cheese	6 potatoes
6 green onions, sliced	½ cup of bacon bits
salt and pepper to taste	

Preheat oven to 375°F. Wash potatoes and place in the oven and cook until the potato skins are crispy and the insides are soft. Cook mac & cheese as directed on the box and set aside. Next, cook your main dish so it will be ready once the potatoes are cooked. Plate your main meal and remove the potatoes from the oven. Slice open the potato to create a wide opening. Add mac & cheese and top with bacon bits and sliced green onion, and salt and pepper to taste.

This spud's for you!

Mac & Cheese Chorizo Bean Cassoulet

From thought to pot to plate: 65 minutes

Serves: 2

Ingredients:

your favorite box of mac & cheese	3 chorizo sausages
4 slices of bacon, chopped	2 cups of white beans, drained
¼ cup of tomato paste	2 carrots, peeled and chopped
1 can of stewed tomatoes	½ cup of white onion, diced
1 stalk of celery, chopped	1 cup of chicken stock
1 bay leaf	5 cloves of garlic, minced
salt and pepper to taste	1 teaspoon of dried rosemary
1 teaspoon of dried thyme	¼ cup of fresh parsley, chopped
dash of olive oil	1 cup of breadcrumbs
1 cup of Parmesan cheese, grated	

Preheat oven to 350°F. Cook mac & cheese as directed on the box. In a large pot, combine the rinsed beans, chicken stock, carrot, onion, celery, garlic and bay leaf and bring to a boil. Skim any impurities that rise to the surface. Simmer gently until beans are tender and cooked through, about 35 minutes. Cook the sausage (casings removed) and bacon over medium heat in a skillet. Add garlic and cook until soft, then the tomato paste, thyme and rosemary. Mix parsley, breadcrumbs and a little olive oil in a separate bowl. Combine the mac & cheese, bean mixture and sausage mixture in a casserole dish and top with parsley breadcrumbs. Bake for about 20 minutes or until bubbling and the top is golden brown. Let stand for 10 minutes before serving.

Enjoy!

Bacon Gruyere Onion Mac & Cheese

From thought to pot to plate: 25 minutes
Serves: 2

Ingredients:

your favorite box of mac & cheese	6 slices of bacon, chopped
salt and pepper to taste	6 green onions, chopped
1 tablespoon of dried parsley	1 cup of Gruyere cheese, grated
2 tablespoons of fresh basil, chopped	pinch of nutmeg
½ cup of sour cream	

Preheat oven to 350°F. Cook the chopped bacon until crispy; set aside on paper towel to drain. Combine the mac & cheese, salt, pepper, sour cream, green onion, parsley nutmeg and basil in a casserole dish. Top with Gruyere and bake for about 15 minutes or until bubbling and the top is golden brown. Let stand for 10 minutes before serving.

Once you have mac, you never go back!

Noodle Notes: ....

....

....

....

....

....

....

....

....

....

....

....

Matterhorn Mac & Cheese

From thought to pot to plate: 45 minutes

Serves: 4

Ingredients:

your favorite box of mac & cheese	4 potatoes, boiled and sliced
2 large white onions, sliced	1 clove of garlic, minced
1 cup of Gruyere cheese, grated	1 cup of heavy cream
salt and pepper to taste	1 tablespoon of butter

Preheat oven to 400°F. Cook mac & cheese as directed on the box. In a skillet, cook the onion in melted butter until soft; add garlic. In a casserole dish layer the mac & cheese, potatoes and onions and repeat. Season with salt and pepper and pour cream evenly over all of the layers, and sprinkle cheese on top. Bake for about 20 minutes or until bubbling and the top is golden brown. Let stand for 10 minutes before serving.

Enjoy!

Mac & Cheese Pepper Chicken Skillet

From thought to pot to plate: 45 minutes

Serves: 4

Ingredients:

two boxes of your favorite mac & cheese	3 chicken breasts, in bite-sized pieces
3 large red peppers, seeded and chopped	1 small white onion, diced
2 cups of your favorite pasta sauce	1 cup of mozzarella, grated
½ cup of Parmesan cheese, grated	dash of olive oil

Preheat oven to 350°F. Cook the mac & cheese as directed on box. Heat olive oil in a large ovenproof skillet over medium heat and cook the chicken; add the peppers and onions cook until soft. Add the mac & cheese and pasta sauce to the skillet. Top with grated mozzarella and Parmesan cheese and place the skillet in the oven for approximately 15 minutes or until bubbling and the top is golden brown.

Enjoy!

Savory Mac & Cream Cheese Pie

From thought to pot to plate: 45 minutes

Serves: 4

Ingredients:

your favorite box of mac & cheese	2 chicken breasts, in bite-sized pieces
1 tablespoon of butter	½ cup of white onion, diced
1 cup of fresh mushrooms, sliced	1 cup of herb garlic cream cheese
½ cup of chicken broth	½ cup of frozen peas, thawed
½ cup of frozen carrots, thawed	1 - 12" piecrust, unbaked
1 egg, beaten	

Preheat oven to 400°F. Cook mac & cheese as directed on the box. In a heated skillet, sauté the onions in melted butter until soft, then stir in the chicken, followed by the mushrooms and cook for 10 minutes. Stir in the cream cheese and chicken broth, followed by the peas and carrots. Combine the mixture with enough mac & cheese to fill the piecrust, and spoon in, ensuring that you have greased the pie dish first. Brush top of chicken and mac mixture with egg, then over with piecrust, gently pressing to seal. Brush top of crust with remaining egg; cut slits in crust for steam to escape and bake for 25 minutes.

Enjoy!

Mac & Cheese Thyme Chicken Bake

From thought to pot to plate: 40 minutes

Serves: 2

Ingredients:

your favorite box of mac & cheese	1lb. of ground chicken
dash of olive oil	½ cup of white onion, diced
1 cup of frozen vegetables, thawed	1 can of cream of celery soup
1 tablespoon of thyme	salt and pepper to taste

Preheat oven to 350°F. Cook mac & cheese as directed on the box. In a skillet, cook the onion and chicken until brown. Add the vegetables, soup, thyme and salt and pepper and stir to combine. Mix well and transfer to a greased casserole dish, along with the mac & cheese. Bake for 20 minutes or until bubbling and heated through.

Enjoy!

Mac & Cheese Stuffed Bell Peppers

From thought to pot to plate: 45 minutes

Serves: 4

Ingredients:

your favorite box of mac & cheese	½ lb. of lean ground beef
8 large red peppers, seeded	2 cloves of garlic, minced
dash of olive oil	salt and pepper to taste
½ cup of white onion, diced	1 tablespoon of parsley, chopped
1 cup of Cheddar cheese, grated	

Preheat oven to 350°F. Cook mac & cheese as directed on the box. In a large skillet, brown the ground beef in olive oil and add the onion and garlic. Mix in parsley and the mac & cheese. Spoon the mixture in each pepper, top with cheese and bake on a sheet pan for 15 minutes or until heated through, bubbling and the top is golden brown.

Enjoy!

Roasted Chicken with Mac & Cheese

From thought to pot to plate: 120 minutes

Serves: 4

Ingredients:

your favorite box of mac & cheese	1 - 5lb. roasting chicken
2 tablespoons of rosemary, chopped	salt and pepper to taste
1 cup of breadcrumbs	1 cup of parsley, chopped
½ cup of Gruyere cheese, grated	2 cloves of garlic, minced
2 tablespoons of butter	

Preheat oven to 375°F. Cook mac & cheese as directed on the box adding garlic, rosemary, salt, pepper, parsley and Gruyere. Fold to combine. Prepare the chicken for roasted by rinsing in water and tucking pats of butter under the skin. Stuff the chicken with the mac & cheese mixture and tie the legs together to keep the stuffing in. Roast for 20 minutes a pound of meat, plus an additional 15 minutes, and five minutes to rest when removed from the oven.

Enjoy!

Noodle Notes: ....

....

....

....

....

....

....

....

....

....

....

....

Mac & Cheese with Peas and Bacon

From thought to pot to plate: 35 minutes

Serves: 2

Ingredients:

your favorite box of mac & cheese	4 slices of bacon, chopped
salt and pepper to taste	2 cloves of garlic, minced
1 cup of frozen peas, thawed	1 teaspoon of dried thyme
dash of olive oil	½ cup of Cheddar cheese, grated
½ cup of white onion, diced	

Preheat oven to 350°F. Cook mac & cheese as directed on the box. Fry bacon in a skillet until crisp; set aside on a paper towel to drain. In the same skillet, sauté the onion, garlic, thyme, salt, pepper and peas until soft. Combine the mac & cheese, bacon and vegetable mixture in a greased casserole dish and cover with the Cheddar. Bake for about 15 minutes or until bubbling and the top is golden brown. Let stand for 10 minutes before serving.

Enjoy!

Noodle Notes: ....

....

....

....

....

....

....

....

....

....

....

....

Mac & Cheese with Scallops

From thought to pot to plate: 45 minutes
Serves: 2

Ingredients:

your favorite box of mac & cheese	½ cup of shallots, diced
2 cloves of garlic, minced	1 cup of frozen peas, thawed
½ cup of chicken broth	4 slices of pancetta, chopped
½ cup of fresh parsley, chopped	juice of one lemon
1 dozen sea scallops, cleaned	2 tablespoons of butter
salt and pepper to taste	

Preheat oven to 350°F. Cook mac & cheese as directed on the box. In a skillet, cook the pancetta until crispy; set aside on paper towel to drain. Sauté the garlic and shallots until soft, add the peas and broth bring to a simmer on low heat. Season the scallops with salt and pepper and in a second pan melt butter with a little lemon juice cook scallops on medium–high heat turning once; should be golden brown on both sides and almost firm to the touch. Combine the pancetta, pea mixture and the scallops and serve on a bed of mac & cheese garnished with the remaining lemon juice and parsley.

Enjoy!

Mac & Cheese
Visits Eastern Europe

Mac & Cheese Chicken Kiev

From thought to pot to plate: 90 minutes
Serves: 4

Ingredients:

your favorite box of mac & cheese	4 chicken breasts
5 tablespoons of butter	2 tablespoons of parsley, chopped
2 teaspoons of dried tarragon	1 clove of garlic, minced
salt and pepper to taste	2 eggs, beaten
½ cup of water	2 cups of panko breadcrumbs
vegetable oil for frying	

Combine butter, parsley, tarragon, garlic, salt and pepper in a food processor. Cover chicken breasts with plastic wrap and pound to 1/8" thickness and season with salt and pepper. Lay one chicken breast on a fresh piece of plastic wrap and spread on a quarter of the butter herb mixture, a scoop of mac & cheese and breadcrumbs sprinkled on top. Using the plastic wrap, roll the breast into a tightly. Repeat process for all of the chicken and refrigerate for about an hour. Cook mac & cheese as directed on the box. Combine the egg and water and place in a shallow bowl. Put the remaining breadcrumbs in another shallow bowl. Heat ½" of vegetable oil in a high- rimmed skillet. Remove the plastic wrap from the chicken and dip each breast in egg, following by the breadcrumbs. Gently place each breast, sealed side down, in the heated oil and cook until golden brown and cooked through. Remove from oil and place on a cooling rack set on a sheet pan to drain.

Enjoy!

Mac & Cheese Rueben

From thought to pot to plate: 40 minutes
Serves: 4

Ingredients:

your favorite box of mac & cheese	1lb. of corned beef, sliced thick
1½ cups of Swiss cheese, grated	2 tablespoons of grainy mustard
1 cup of sauerkraut, drained	1 tbsp. of 1000 Island-style dressing
1 cup of rye chips, crumbled	

Preheat oven to 350°F. Cook mac & cheese as directed on the box. Combine the mustard, corned beef and sauerkraut with the mac & cheese. Transfer to a casserole dish and top with the crumbled rye chips and Swiss cheese. Bake for about 15 minutes or until bubbling and the top is golden brown. Let stand for 10 minutes before serving. Before serving, drizzle the top with creamy salad dressing.

Oy vey!

Mac & Cheese with Ukrainian Sausage

From thought to pot to plate: 25 minutes
Serves: 2

Ingredients:

your favorite box mac & cheese	dash of olive oil
½lb. of Ukrainian sausage	½ cup of white onion, diced
½ a green pepper, chopped	6 cherry tomatoes cut in half

Cook mac & cheese as directed on the box. In a skillet, add olive oil and brown the sausage (casings removed), green pepper and onion until soft. Stir mixture into the mac & cheese and top with cherry tomatoes.

Enjoy!

Mac & Cheese Cabbage Rolls

From thought to pot to plate: 90 minutes

Serves: 6

Ingredients:

your favorite box of mac & cheese	1lb. of lean ground beef
18 Savoy cabbage leaves	½ cup of white onion, diced
dash of olive oil	salt and pepper to taste
½ cup of carrot, grated	1 tablespoon of paprika
2 teaspoons of celery salt	1 small can of tomato sauce
1 small can of diced tomatoes	2 teaspoons of sugar
2 tablespoons of vinegar	1 small jar of sauerkraut

Preheat oven to 375°F. Cook mac & cheese as directed on the box. In a large skillet, cook the ground beef and sauté the onion and carrot until soft over medium heat, followed by the paprika and celery salt. Set meat mixture aside. Bring a large pot of salted water to a boil. Peel away cabbage leaves carefully and blanche in boiling water until pliable (for about 2 minutes), place blanched leaves on a sheet pan and cut out the stem. Place a spoonful of the meat mixture on a leaf, following by a spoonful of mac & cheese. Roll leaf as tightly as possible without tearing. If necessary, secure the roll with a toothpick. Repeat process with remaining cabbage leaves. Spread half of the sauerkraut in the bottom of a large casserole dish. Place the cabbage rolls on top, and then layer on the remaining sauerkraut and pour a combination of the tomato sauce, diced tomatoes and juice, vinegar and sugar on top. Cover the dish and bake for an hour at 375°F, then reduce oven temperature to 350°F and cook another 15 minutes. Remove from the oven and let stand for 15 minutes and remove toothpicks before serving.

Enjoy!

Gouda Spinach Salami Mac & Cheese

From thought to pot to plate: 40 minutes

Serves: 2

Ingredients:

your favorite box of mac & cheese	½ cup of red onion, diced
dash of olive oil	salt and pepper to taste
2 cloves of garlic, minced	1½ cups of Italian salami, chopped
1 bunch of fresh spinach	2 cups of smoked Gouda, grated
2 teaspoons of red pepper flakes	1 cup of fresh parsley, chopped
½ cup of breadcrumbs	

Preheat oven to 350°F. Cook mac & cheese as directed on the box. In a large skillet, soften the onion and garlic in olive oil. Rinse, stem and chop the spinach. Add the salami, spinach, red pepper flakes and parsley. Fold mixture with the mac & cheese in a greased casserole dish with the fresh spinach, salt and pepper. Top with Gouda and breadcrumbs and bake for about 20 minutes or until bubbling and the top is golden brown. Let stand for 10 minutes before serving.

Gouda, get it? Enjoy!

Cabbage and Prosciutto Mac & Cheese

From thought to pot to plate: 35 minutes

Serves: 2

Ingredients:

your favorite box of mac & cheese	½ head of white cabbage, chopped
dash of olive oil	2 cloves of garlic, minced
1½ teaspoon of red pepper flakes	3oz. of prosciutto, cut in strips
¼ cup of Parmesan cheese, grated	salt and pepper to taste

Cook mac & cheese as directed on the box. In a pot of boiling salted water, cook cabbage for 4 minutes until softened and remove from the water. Heat oil in a skillet over medium heat, add the prosciutto and cook until crispy, then stir in the minced garlic, cabbage, pepper flakes, salt and pepper. Combine the mac & cheese with the cabbage and prosciutto, grated Parmesan cheese and stir to combine. Serve.

Enjoy!

Mac & Cheese with Kielbasa and Sauerkraut

From thought to pot to plate: 35 minutes

Serves: 2

Ingredients:

your favorite box of mac & cheese	dash of olive oil
1lb. of kielbasa sausage, sliced ½" thick	8 oz. of sauerkraut, drained
1 tablespoon of Dijon mustard	pepper to taste

Cook mac & cheese as directed on the box. Heat oil in a skillet on medium heat, add sausage and cook until brown. Stir in the sauerkraut, mustard and pepper and cook for another 3 minutes. Remove from heat and stir into the mac & cheese. Serve.

Enjoy!

Mac & Cheese Beef Stroganoff

From thought to pot to plate: 40 minutes
Serves: 2

Ingredients:

box of mac & white Cheddar cheese	1lb. of lean ground beef
½ cup of butter	½ cup of white onion, diced
2 cloves of garlic, minced	2 tablespoons of flour
salt and pepper to taste	1 cup of fresh mushrooms, sliced
1 can of cream of chicken soup	1 cup of sour cream
1 cup of fresh parsley, chopped	

Cook mac & cheese as directed on the box. Sauté the white onion in butter until tender; stir in beef, garlic, flour, salt, pepper and mushrooms, and cook for a further five minutes. Add soup and simmer uncovered for ten minutes. Stir sour cream into the meat mixture and sprinkle with parsley. Serve on top of a bed of mac & cheese.

Beef stroganoff? Don't mind if I do!

Noodle Notes: ....

....

....

....

....

....

....

....

....

....

....

....

124

Mac & Cheese Perogies

From thought to pot to plate: 45 minutes
Serves: 4

Ingredients:

your favorite box of mac & cheese	your favorite perogy dough
2 medium sized potatoes	1 cup of Cheddar cheese, grated
½ cup of white onion, diced	salt and pepper to taste
3 strips of bacon, chopped	½ cup of sour cream
5 green onions, sliced	

Cook mac & cheese as directed on the box. Set a pot of water on to boil to cook peeled potatoes, then mash. Combine the mashed potatoes, Cheddar cheese, onion, salt and pepper with the mac & cheese. Roll out perogy dough to 1/8" thickness and cut into 3" rounds. Place heaping teaspoon of the mac & cheese potato mixture on the dough, fold over and crimp edges to seal. Cook the bacon until crispy and set aside on paper towel to drain. Boil the perogies in water until they float (approximately 2 minutes). Drain finished perogies and serve topped with bacon, sour cream and green onion.

Enjoy!

Noodle Notes: ....
....
....
....
....
....
....
....
....
....
....

Mac-erranean

Classic Moussaka Mac & Cheese

From thought to pot to plate: 45 minutes
Serves: 4

Ingredients:

your favorite box of mac & cheese	2 eggplants, peeled, sliced
1lb. of ground lamb	1 can of stewed tomatoes
1 cup of white onion, diced	3 cloves of garlic, minced
½ teaspoon of cinnamon	¼ teaspoon of allspice, ground
½ cup of water	2 tablespoons of tomato paste
1 teaspoon of butter	½ cup of red wine
1 cup of breadcrumbs	1 carrot, peeled and diced
1 cup of button mushrooms, sliced	¼ teaspoon of cayenne pepper
3 tablespoons of flour	½ cup of Cheddar cheese, grated
dash of olive oil	½ cup of milk
salt and pepper to taste	

Preheat oven to 350°F. Cook mac & cheese as directed on the box. Heat the olive oil in a skillet on medium high heat and sauté the sliced eggplant on both sides until lightly browned. Set aside on a paper towel. Cook the lamb in the skillet, along with the carrots and onions. Add the water, tomatoes, garlic, mushrooms, cinnamon, cayenne pepper, allspice, salt and pepper. Add the tomato paste and red wine and simmer for about 10 minutes. Melt butter in a second pan and gradually add the flour to make a roux. Add milk, salt, pepper and cheese. In a casserole dish, layer eggplant, a layer of meat and a layer of mac & cheese, and repeat until the dish is full. Cover with cheese sauce and breadcrumbs. Bake for about 25 minutes or until bubbling and the top is golden brown. Let stand for 10 minutes before serving.

Smash some dishes on the floor already people!

Sicilian Mac & Cheese Pizza

From thought to pot to plate: 50 minutes

Serves: 2

Ingredients:

your favorite box of mac & cheese	1 egg, beaten
2 tablespoons of olive oil	½ cup of white onion, diced
1 can of plum tomatoes, drained	1 cup of Provolone cheese, grated
1 can of sardines, drained	

Preheat oven to 350°F. Cook mac & cheese as directed on the box and stir in the egg. Press mixture on to the bottom of a greased 12" pizza pan and bake for 5 minutes. Heat oil in pan over medium heat; add onion and sauté until translucent. Add chopped tomatoes and reduce heat to low, simmer until desired consistency for pizza sauce, stirring occasionally. Top bake pasta with tomato sauce and cheese, bake for another 10 minutes; remove from oven and place the sardines on top like hands on a clock. Return to oven for 5 minutes longer until heated through and cheese has melted and is golden brown.

Enjoy!

Noodle Notes: ....

....

....

....

....

....

....

....

....

....

....

....

Chicken Souvlaki Mac & Cheese

From thought to pot to plate: 45 minutes

Serves: 4

Ingredients:

your favorite box of mac & cheese	3 chicken breasts, in bite-sized pieces
juice of two lemons	dash of olive oil
1 teaspoon of dried oregano	1 teaspoon of dried mint
½ cup of red onion, diced	½ cucumber, peeled and chopped
½ cup of tzatziki (Recipes Reference)	4 pitas
1 tomato, chopped	1 cup of romaine lettuce, shredded
2 red peppers chopped	¼ cup of red wine vinegar
3 cloves of garlic, minced	salt and pepper to taste

In large bowl, toss together chicken, lemon juice, oil, garlic, mint, oregano, red wine vinegar, salt and pepper; let marinate for ten minutes in the refrigerator. Cook mac & cheese as directed on the box. Thread chicken, peppers and onion onto 4 metal skewers. Place skewers on BBQ and cook thoroughly - about 10 minutes. Spread tzatziki over one side of each pita. Push chicken and onion off skewers onto pitas and top with a scoop of mac & cheese, tomato, cucumber and lettuce. Garnish with squeeze of fresh lemon.

Enjoy!

Spanakopita Mac & Cheese Muffins

From thought to pot to plate: 35 minutes

Serves: 6

Ingredients:

your favorite box of mac & cheese	1 teaspoon of butter
3 cups of fresh spinach	¾ cup of feta cheese, crumbled
1 cup of flour	3 cloves of garlic, minced
salt and pepper to taste	½ teaspoon of baking powder

Preheat oven to 350°F. Cook mac & cheese as directed on the box. Grease a 6-cup muffin tin with butter. Rinse, dry, stem and chop the spinach. Fold spinach, feta, flour, baking powder, garlic and salt and pepper to mac and cheese. Divide mixture evenly in muffin cups and bake for 20 to 25 minutes or until a knife inserted in centre comes out clean. Let stand for five minutes before serving.

Enjoy!

Noodle Notes: ....

....

....

....

....

....

....

....

....

....

....

....

....

My Big Fat Toga Mac & Cheese

From thought to pot to plate: 35 minutes
Serves: 2

Ingredients:

your favorite box of mac & cheese	juice of two lemons
1 teaspoon of dried oregano	2 cups of feta, crumbled
3 red peppers chopped	½ cup of Kalamata olives, pitted
½ cup of fresh parsley, chopped	dash of olive oil
1/3 cup of pepperoncini*, chopped	dash of pepper

Cook mac & cheese as directed on the box. Add *olive* the other ingredients to a skillet on low heat until the feta and peppers soften and the parsley wilts, folding gently. Serve on a bed of mac & cheese.

* Tuscan or sweet Italian pepper

Get it? Olive the other ingredients? Opa!

Noodle Notes: ....

....

....

....

....

....

....

....

....

....

....

....

Mac & Cheese Tabouli

From thought to pot to plate: 55 minutes
Serves: 4

Ingredients:

your favorite box of mac & cheese	2 cups of cracked wheat (bulgur)
2 cups of boiling water	1 cucumber, peeled and chopped
2 small tomatoes, chopped	4 green onions, sliced
½ cup of fresh mint, chopped	3 cups of fresh parsley, chopped
1 clove of garlic, minced	juice of two lemons
salt and pepper to taste	1 teaspoon of olive oil

Soak the cracked wheat in the boiling water until the water is absorbed – about 30 minutes, drain any excess. Cook mac & cheese as directed on the box and place in refrigerator to cool. Combine the cucumber, tomatoes, green onion, mint, parsley, garlic, salt, pepper and lemon juice with the olive oil. Combine with the chilled mac & cheese. Serve cold.

Enjoy!

Noodle Notes: ....

....

....

....

....

....

....

....

....

....

....

Mac & Cheese Falafel

From thought to pot to plate: 45 minutes

Serves: 4

Ingredients:

your favorite box of mac & cheese	1 can of garbanzo beans, drained
1 cup of white onion, diced	3 cloves of garlic, minced
3 tablespoons of parsley, chopped	1 teaspoon of coriander
1 teaspoon of cumin	2 tablespoons of flour
salt and pepper to taste	1 teaspoon of baking powder
juice of one lemon	vegetable oil for frying
1 large radish, sliced	8 pita pockets
1 cup of lettuce, shredded	1 cup of tomato, diced
½ cup of red onion, diced	1 cup of tzatziki (Recipes Reference)

Cook mac & cheese as directed on the box. In a food processor coarsely chop together the rinsed chickpeas, onion, parsley and garlic. Add the flour, cumin, baking powder, salt, pepper and lemon juice; pulse until just blended. Shape by heaping 1 tablespoon of the mixture into balls, flatten to ½" thick, and arrange on a sheet pan to be covered and refrigerated for about half an hour. Pour enough oil in a heavy skillet – about ¼" worth – and on medium high. Fry the falafels, turning until golden. Transfer to paper towel with a slotted spoon to drain. Set out the falafel, pita pockets, along with the lettuce, radish, tzatziki, tomato, red onion and mac & cheese so guests can garnish their own falafel.

Feel awful? Have one of these!

Marrakesh Mac & Cheese

From thought to pot to plate: 35 minutes

Serves: 2

Ingredients:

your favorite box of mac & cheese	4 green onions, sliced
4 cloves of garlic, minced	2 teaspoons of Ancho chile powder
1 teaspoon of ground cumin	1 teaspoon of ground coriander
1 teaspoon of lemon zest	2 teaspoons of fresh parsley, chopped
2 teaspoons of fresh mint, chopped	1 teaspoon of fresh cilantro, chopped
2 tablespoons of butter	salt and pepper to taste

Cook mac & cheese as directed on the box. Make herb butter by combining the remaining ingredients in a bowl with butter. Toss the herbed butter with the mac & cheese and serve.

Enjoy!

Noodle Notes: ....
....
....
....
....
....
....
....
....
....
....
....
....

Mac & Cheese Lemon Herb Chicken

From thought to pot to plate: 90 minutes
Serves: 6

Ingredients:

your favorite box of mac & cheese	1 whole roasting chicken
1 cup of cream cheese	2 teaspoons of rosemary
salt and pepper to taste	3 cloves of garlic
2 tablespoons of lemon juice	2 teaspoons of Italian dressing
6 slices of bacon, chopped	2 green onions, chopped

Preheat oven to 375°F. Cook mac & cheese as directed on the box. Mix cream cheese, garlic, rosemary, salt and pepper together. Starting at the neck of the chicken, thighs and legs, carefully spoon the mixture under the skin, careful not to tear it. Place chicken in a shallow roasting pan and brush with 2 teaspoons of the Italian dressing and lemon juice. Cook the bacon and green onions and combine with the mac & cheese. Serve sliced chicken on a bed of the mac & cheese, drizzling drippings on top.

Enjoy!

Noodle Notes: ....

....

....

....

....

....

....

....

....

....

....

134

Chicken and Artichoke Mac & Cheese

From thought to pot to plate: 40 minutes
Serves: 4

Ingredients:

your favorite box of mac & cheese	4 chicken breasts, in bite-sized pieces
dash of olive oil	1 small red onion, sliced
1 jar of marinated artichokes, drained	3 cloves of garlic, minced
salt and pepper to taste	1 cup of fresh mushrooms, sliced
1 tablespoon of capers	1 cup of white wine
1 cup of Swiss cheese, grated	1 cup of parsley, chopped
1 tablespoon of lemon juice	

Preheat oven to 350°F. Cook mac & cheese as directed on the box. In a skillet, heat olive oil and cook the chicken, onion, garlic and mushrooms; adding white wine and allowing it to evaporate. Once cooked, combine the mac & cheese, chicken mixture, salt, pepper, quartered artichokes, capers, lemon juice and parsley in a casserole dish. Top with Swiss cheese and bake for about 15 minutes or until bubbling and the top is golden brown. Let stand for 10 minutes before serving.

Enjoy!

Noodle Notes: ....
....
....
....
....
....
....
....
....
....

Mac & Cheese Patitsio

From thought to pot to plate: 50 minutes
Serves: 4

Ingredients:

2 boxes of your favorite mac & cheese	2lb. of lean ground beef
3 cloves of garlic, minced	1 cup of white onion, diced
1 can of stewed tomatoes, drained	1 can of tomato paste
1 teaspoon of nutmeg	1 teaspoon of dried oregano
1 teaspoon of cinnamon	salt and pepper to taste
1 cup of mozzarella cheese, grated	3 cups of milk
4 tablespoons of butter	4 tablespoons of flour
4 egg yolks	

Preheat oven to 350°F. Cook mac & cheese as directed on the box. Brown the meat in a skillet, along with the onion. Mix in stewed tomato, tomato paste, garlic, cinnamon, oregano, salt and pepper. Simmer until sauce has thickened. Melt butter on low heat in a second pan. Stir in flour and blend. Whisk in milk until sauce thickens and remove from heat. Add nutmeg, mozzarella, salt, pepper and the egg yolks. Assemble the patitsio in a large casserole dish; layer half of the mac & cheese evenly along the bottom, followed by a layer of the meat sauce, and a second layer of mac & cheese. Top with the béchamel (cream sauce) and bake for about 30 minutes or until bubbling and the top is golden brown. Let stand for 10 minutes before serving.

Enjoy!

Greek Mac & Cheese Dinner

From thought to pot to plate: 35 minutes
Serves: 4

Ingredients:

2 boxes of your favorite mac & cheese	dash of olive oil
2 cloves of garlic, minced	½ cup of red onion, diced
1 green pepper, chopped	3 slices of back bacon, chopped
½ cup of Feta cheese, crumbled	½ cup of Kalamata olives, pitted
dash of red pepper flakes	1 can of tomatoes, not drained; chopped
4 tablespoons of tomato paste	1 teaspoon of dried oregano
salt and pepper to taste	

Cook mac & cheese as directed on the box. Cook bacon until crispy and set aside on paper towel to drain. Sauté garlic, onion and green pepper in olive oil until soft; then add the most of the bacon, most of the feta, chopped olives and chili flakes and continue to cook for about 3 minutes. Add tomatoes and tomato paste and season with salt, pepper and oregano. Combine mixture with the cooked mac & cheese in a serving dish garnished with reserved bacon bits and feta.

Opa!

Noodle Notes:

Hummus and Pita Mac & Cheese

From thought to pot to plate: 45 minutes
Serves: 2

Ingredients:

your favorite box of mac & cheese	1 can of garbanzo beans, drained
2 tablespoons of olive oil	5 tablespoons of lemon juice
2 tablespoons of tahini	4 cloves of garlic, minced
salt and pepper to taste	1 teaspoon of cumin
½ cup of fresh parsley, chopped	pinch of paprika
pita chips	

Cook mac & cheese as directed on the box. In a food processor, combine the rinsed garbanzo beans, olive oil, lemon juice, tahini, garlic, salt, pepper and cumin. Pulse to combine. In a serving bowl, spread the mac & cheese on the bottom and top with hummus. Garnish with paprika, parsley, more lemon juice and pita chips.

Enjoy!

Noodle Notes: ....

....

....

....

....

....

....

....

....

....

Mediterranean Mac & Cheese

From thought to pot to plate: 45 minutes

Serves: 2

Ingredients:

your favorite box of mac & cheese	juice of one lemon
2 cloves of garlic, minced	1 cup of Kalamata olives, pitted
1 cup of feta, crumbled	½ cup of marinated sun-dried tomatoes
2 cups of shrimp, peeled and deveined	½ cup of red onion, diced
1 teaspoon of fresh rosemary, chopped	2 teaspoons of butter
salt and pepper to taste	

Cook mac & cheese as directed on the box. In a heated skillet, cook the shrimp until opaque. Combine the mac & cheese, pitted olives, feta, sun-dried tomatoes, salt, pepper, rosemary and onion together on platter and serve, drizzled with lemon juice.

Lie back and eat grapes after this classic mac dish and pretend you are looking at the Adriatic or… Adonis.

Chickpea and Parsley Mac & Cheese

From thought to pot to plate: 45 minutes

Serves: 2

Ingredients:

your favorite box of mac & cheese	2 cups of chickpeas (garbanzo beans)
½ cup of parsley, chopped	1 cup of Cheddar cheese, grated
1 cup of salsa	salt and pepper to taste

Preheat oven to 350°F. Cook mac & cheese as directed on the box. Combine the chickpeas, salsa, most of the Cheddar, parsley, salt and pepper in a greased casserole dish. Top with the remaining cheese and bake for about 15 minutes or until bubbling and the top is golden brown. Let stand for 10 minutes before serving.

Enjoy!

Tzatziki Mac & Cheese Salad

From thought to pot to plate: 30 minutes
Serves: 2

Ingredients:

your favorite box of mac & cheese	3 cucumbers, peeled, grated
3 cloves of garlic, minced	½ cup of red onion, diced
½ cup of Greek yogurt	1 tablespoon of fresh dill, chopped
1 teaspoon of lemon juice	salt and pepper to taste

Cook mac & cheese as directed on the box. Set aside in the fridge to chill. Combine the cored and grated cucumber, garlic, onion, yogurt, dill, lemon, lemon juice, salt and pepper and stir in the mac & cheese once chilled. Serve cold as a side dish.

Opa!

Artichoke Olive Mac & Feta Cheese

From thought to pot to plate: 40 minutes
Serves: 2

Ingredients:

your favorite box of mac & cheese	5 cloves of garlic, minced
½ cup of red onion, diced	2 teaspoons of dried oregano
dash of olive oil	pepper to taste
1½ cups of feta, crumbled	1 red pepper, chopped
1 cup of Kalamata olives, pitted	1 can of artichoke hearts, drained

Preheat oven to 400°F. Cook mac & cheese as directed on the box. Sauté the garlic and red onion in olive oil until soft, then remove from heat. Add the mac & cheese with the rest of the ingredients in a casserole dish to bake for approximately 15 minutes until bubbling and heated through.

Enjoy!

140

Mac & Cheese with Lentils

From thought to pot to plate: 35 minutes

Serves: 2

Ingredients:

your favorite box of mac & cheese	1 small can of lentils, drained
1 red pepper, chopped	½ cup of broccoli, cut into florets
1 tablespoon of butter	½ cup of milk
½ cup of breadcrumbs	1 cup of Cheddar cheese, grated

Preheat oven to 350°F. Cook mac & cheese as directed on the box. Combine mac & cheese, vegetables, lentils, milk and half of the grated Cheddar cheese; put in a casserole dish and top with remaining cheese and breadcrumbs. Bake for about 20 minutes or until bubbling and the top is golden brown. Let stand for 10 minutes before serving.

Enjoy!

Noodle Notes: ....

....

....

....

....

....

....

....

....

....

....

....

....

....

Sun-Dried Tomato Chicken Mac & Cheese

From thought to pot to plate: 45 minutes
Serves: 4

Ingredients:

your favorite box of mac & cheese	4 slices of bacon, chopped
4 chicken breasts	½ cup of sun-dried tomatoes, chopped
½ cup of sun-dried tomato dressing	1 teaspoon of dried basil
2 large tomatoes, chopped	¼ cup of Parmesan cheese, grated
salt and pepper to taste	

Cook mac & cheese as directed on the box. Cook the chopped bacon in a large skillet until crisp then set aside on paper towel to drain. Clean the skillet. Cook the chicken on medium heat for two minutes per side or until browned. Pour ½ cup of dressing over chicken and sprinkle with sun-dried tomatoes and basil. Reduce heat to low and cook for approximately 10 more minutes, turning the chicken evenly. Put chicken on a large serving platter - with room for the mac & cheese - and set aside, covered with foil to stay warm. Put the other half of the dressing in the skillet with the tomatoes and stir on medium heat, adding salt and pepper, and bacon once hot. Spoon the mixture over the chicken and top with Parmesan. Place the mac & cheese on the platter and get ready to impress people!

Enjoy!

East Meets West Mac & Cheese

Pad Thai Mac & Cheese

From thought to pot to plate: 35 minutes

Serves: 2

Ingredients:

your favorite box of mac & cheese	2 chicken breasts, in bite-sized pieces
1 cup of shrimp, peeled and deveined	1 egg, beaten
1 cup of medium tofu, cubed	2 cups of fresh bean sprouts
3 tablespoons of soy sauce	3 cloves of garlic, minced
2 fresh Thai chilies, seeded and diced	4 green onions, sliced
1 cup of fresh coriander, chopped	½ cup of unsalted peanuts, crushed
¼ cup of chicken stock	1 tablespoon of tamarind paste
¼ cup of warm water	1 tablespoon of fish sauce
2 teaspoons of sambal oeleck	2 tablespoons of fresh lime juice
1 red pepper, seeded and diced	cooking oil
1 lime, cut into wedges	

Cook mac & cheese as directed on the box. In small bowl, mix together the chilies, fish sauce, lime juice, soy sauce and tamarind paste and coat the chicken with it. In wok, heat one teaspoon of oil over medium-high heat; stir-fry the chicken mixture, garlic, sambal oeleck and red pepper until soft. Add chicken stock and stir-fry shrimp until pink, about 2 minutes. Add fish sauce mixture and bring to boil; reduce heat to medium. Stir in egg until sauce is thickened, for about one minute. Add tofu, bean sprouts, green onions and chopped coriander; toss and stir-fry until tender, for about 3 minutes. Garnish with peanuts, coriander and lime wedges on a bed of mac & cheese.

Enjoy!

Mac & Cheese Sushi

From thought to pot to plate: 105 minutes
Serves: 2

Ingredients:

your favorite box of mac & cheese	½lb. of lean ground beef
2 sheets of nori (edible seaweed)	dash of olive oil
2 tablespoons of teriyaki sauce	

Cook mac & cheese as directed on the box. Brown the beef in a skillet in olive oil and season with teriyaki sauce. Set the nori sheets out on a flat work surface. Once mac is cool, roll onto the nori - about ¼" thick. Cover with the cooked ground beef. Roll each sheet and let set in the refrigerator for about an hour. Serve drizzled with teriyaki sauce and cut at about ½" intervals. Serve cold.

And you thought sushi was just fish?

Chopsticks Mac & Cheese

From thought to pot to plate: 25 minutes
Serves: 4

Ingredients:

your favorite box of mac & cheese	3 chicken breasts, in bite-sized pieces
2 cups of frozen Oriental style vegetables	1 can of water chestnuts, drained
3 green onions, chopped	2 tablespoons of soy sauce
½ teaspoon of sesame oil	dash of olive oil

Cook mac & cheese as directed on the box. Add the frozen vegetables for the last 2 minutes of cooking time; then drain the pasta and the vegetables together. In a large skillet sauté the chicken in a dash of olive oil until cooked through, then add the soy sauce, sesame oil and water chestnuts. Serve chicken mixture on a bed of mac & cheese, topped with sliced green onion.

Enjoy!

Mac & Cheese Steak Stir-Fry

From thought to pot to plate: 40 minutes

Serves: 2

Ingredients:

your favorite box of mac & cheese	1lb. of beef sirloin, in bite-sized pieces
2 medium sized potatoes, peeled	3 carrots, peeled and chopped
1 teaspoon of olive oil	¼ cup of water
2 cups of fresh mushrooms, sliced	1 cup of white onion, diced
1 cup of broccoli florets	¼ cup of vinaigrette
salt and pepper to taste	sesame seeds

Cook mac & cheese as directed on the box. In a heated skillet, sauté the beef, mushrooms and onions in the olive oil for 2 or 3 minutes or until brown. Remove from skillet and set aside. Using the same skillet, add water, chopped potatoes and carrots and bring to a boil, cover and let simmer on low heat for 15 minutes or until tender, adding broccoli for the last minute. Add vegetables to mac and cheese along with the beef and mushroom mixture. Pour in vinaigrette and stir over medium to high heat until heated through Serve on a bed of mac & cheese, garnished with sesame seeds.

Chopsticks optional!

Kung Pao Chicken Mac & Cheese

From thought to pot to plate: 35 minutes

Serves: 2

Ingredients:

your favorite box of mac & cheese	2 chicken breasts, in bite-sized pieces
2 tablespoons of soy sauce	2 dried red chilies, diced
1 tbsp. of fresh ginger, minced	1 teaspoon of sesame oil
1 teaspoon of cornstarch	1 teaspoon of honey
1 teaspoon of vegetable oil	1 red pepper, seeded chopped
4 green onions, sliced	1 cup of cashews, unsalted
1 tablespoon of chili-garlic sauce	1 cup of fresh bean sprouts

Cook mac & cheese as directed on the box. Combine one tablespoon of soy sauce with the ginger, honey and sesame oil in a medium sized bowl and add the chicken. Stir to coat, then stir in the cornstarch and set aside. Combine the remaining soy sauce with chili-garlic sauce in a small bowl. Heat oil in a wok and add the marinated chicken, stir-frying until cooked. Add the chilies, pepper, green onion, and soy/chili mixture. Serve on a bed of mac & cheese garnished with fresh bean sprouts and cashews.

Enjoy!

Thai One On Mac & Cheese

From thought to pot to plate: 40 minutes

Serves: 2

Ingredients:

your favorite box of mac & cheese	1 tablespoon of vegetable oil
2 red peppers, chopped	4 cloves of garlic, minced
1 Thai red chili, sliced	1 carrot, peeled, sliced
1 cup of fresh cilantro, chopped	1 teaspoon of fresh ginger, grated
2 baby bok choy, chopped	1 cup of fresh basil, chopped
1 can of bamboo shoots, drained	1 teaspoon of fish sauce
3 teaspoons of fresh lime juice	2 tablespoons of soy sauce
1 can of coconut milk	

Cook mac & cheese as directed on the box. In a large wok heat the vegetable oil and stir-fry the red peppers, garlic, chili, carrot, cilantro, ginger, bok choy, basil and bamboo shoots. Add the fish sauce, lime juice, soy sauce and coconut milk. Serve on a large platter on a bed of mac & cheese, garnished with chopped cilantro.

Enjoy!

Noodle Notes: ....
....
....
....
....
....
....
....
....
....

Oyakodon Mac & Cheese

From thought to pot to plate: 40 minutes
Serves: 2

Ingredients:

your favorite box of mac & cheese	2 chicken breasts, in bite-sized pieces
1 cup of fish stock	3 tablespoons of soy sauce
2 tablespoons of mirin	2 tablespoons of sugar
½ cup of white onion, diced	3 eggs, beaten
3 green onions, sliced	

Cook mac & cheese as directed on the box. Cook the chicken and onion in fish sauce in a skillet on medium heat; then add soy sauce, mirin and sugar to bring mixture to a boil. Add the eggs and sprinkle green onions on top. Cover and cook on low-medium heat until the egg is set. Serve on a bed of mac & cheese.

Enjoy!

Miso Lucky Mac & Cheese

From thought to pot to plate: 25 minutes
Serves: 2

Ingredients:

your favorite box of mac & cheese	1 tablespoon of butter
¼ cup of miso paste	½ cup of Tahini
½ teaspoon of sesame seeds	1 green onion, sliced

Cook mac & cheese as directed on the box. Melt butter in a skillet and add the miso, whisking in. After about two minutes add the tahini and whisk to combine. Fold into the mac & cheese and serve garnished with sesame seeds and green onion.

Miso enjoy!

Thai Peanut Chicken Mac & Cheese

From thought to pot to plate: 45 minutes

Serves: 4

Ingredients:

your favorite box of mac & cheese	3 chicken breasts, in bite-sized pieces
3 tablespoons of soy sauce	2 tablespoons of smooth peanut butter
2 teaspoons of white vinegar	1 teaspoon of rice vinegar
1 cup of broccoli, cut into florets	1 teaspoon of cayenne pepper
4 cloves of garlic, minced	2 tablespoons of fresh ginger, grated
4 green onions, sliced	½ cup of unsalted peanuts, crushed

Cook mac & cheese as directed on the box. In a small bowl, stir together the soy sauce, peanut butter, vinegar and cayenne pepper. Set aside. Heat oil in a wok over high heat. Add chicken, garlic and ginger and stir constantly for about 5 minutes. Reduce heat to medium and add broccoli, peanuts and the peanut butter mixture. Stir frequently for 5 minutes until broccoli is tender and chicken is cooked. Serve on a bed of mac & cheese garnished with green onions.

Enjoy!

Sweet and Sour Chicken Mac & Cheese

From thought to pot to plate: 45 minutes
Serves: 4

Ingredients:

your favorite box of mac & cheese	4 chicken breasts, in bite-sized pieces
1 egg white	2 tablespoons of cornstarch
2 tablespoons of flour	salt and pepper to taste
dash of olive oil	1/3 cup of chicken broth
3 tablespoons of ketchup	1 tablespoon of soy sauce
1 tablespoon of rice vinegar	2 teaspoons of fresh ginger, grated
½ cup of white onion, diced	1 red pepper, seeded and chopped
1 green pepper, seeded and chopped	1 can of pineapple chunks, drained
¼ cup of pineapple juice	2 tablespoons of sugar

Cook mac & cheese as directed on the box. Combine the chicken, egg white, cornstarch, flour, salt and pepper and cool in the refrigerator for ten minutes. In a large skillet heat oil over medium-high heat, stir-fry chicken, reserving the marinade. Set the cooked chicken aside. Add the broth, 1/3 cup of water, ketchup, pineapple juice, soy sauce, vinegar, ginger and sugar to the marinade and whisk to combine. Stir-fry the peppers and onion until tender. Add the chicken, pineapple and marinade to the wok and stir-fry until sauce thickened and the chicken is coated. Serve on a bed of mac & cheese.

Enjoy!

Mac & Cheese with Wicked Asian Greens

From thought to pot to plate: 35 minutes

Serves: 2

Ingredients:

your favorite box of mac & cheese	½ cup of white onion, diced
4 cloves of garlic, minced	5 baby bok choy, chopped
½ cup of frozen peas, thawed	1 can of water chestnuts, drained
2 stalks of celery, chopped	3 green onions, sliced
juice of one lemon	1 tablespoon of soy sauce
1 teaspoon of fresh ginger, grated	2 cups of pea shoots
½ teaspoon of sesame oil	1 cup of napa cabbage, shredded
1 cup of broccoli florets	1 cup of mizuna, chopped
1 teaspoon of rice vinegar	1 teaspoon of cooking oil

Cook mac & cheese as directed on the box. In a large wok, heat the cooking oil on medium heat and cook the onion and garlic, followed by the vegetables. Add the water chestnuts, sesame oil, soy sauce, lemon juice and ginger. Cook until wilted; for about 3 minutes. Serve greens on a bed of mac & cheese.

Knife and forks or chopsticks? You decide.

Spicy Chicken Stir-Fry Mac & Cheese

From thought to pot to plate: 45 minutes
Serves: 2

Ingredients:

your favorite box of mac & cheese	1 chicken breast, in bite-sized pieces
1 teaspoon of Worcestershire sauce	2 cloves of garlic, minced
salt and pepper to taste	1 teaspoon of cornstarch
1 tablespoon of water	dash of olive oil
2 red peppers, chopped	2 chili peppers, diced
1 tablespoon of sesame seeds	1 cup of white onion, diced
3 baby bok choy, chopped	2 stems of celery, chopped
2 tablespoons of soy sauce	

Combine the chicken, Worcestershire sauce, garlic, salt, pepper and chili peppers and marinate for 30 minutes in the refrigerator. Cook mac & cheese as directed on the box. In a large skillet, heat the olive oil and add the chopped red pepper, diced white onion, chopped celery and baby bok choy and cook on medium heat until soft. Remove vegetables from skillet and set aside. Put chicken and marinade in the skillet and sauté until cooked. Combine cornstarch with a tablespoon of water until blended, then add to the chicken and cook until sauce thickens. Add the cooked vegetables and sesame seeds and stir-fry together. Serve on a bed of mac & cheese.

Spicy enough for ya? Enjoy!

Sesame Beef with Broccoli Mac & Cheese

From thought to pot to plate: 25 minutes

Serves: 2

Ingredients:

your favorite box of mac & cheese	1lb. of rib eye steak, cut in strips
dash of olive oil	1 clove of garlic, minced
1 teaspoon of sesame seeds	dash of olive oil
2 green onions, sliced	2 cups of broccoli, cut into florets
1 tablespoon of cornstarch	½ teaspoon of sesame oil
1 cup of water	salt and pepper to taste

Cook mac & cheese as directed on the box. Heat olive oil in a wok on medium heat. Cook the steak to your liking - about 4 minutes -and set aside, cover to keep warm. Add broccoli, garlic and green onion to the wok, stir-fry until tender crisp. Pour in cornstarch and water mixture and stir until slightly thickened; season with salt and pepper to taste. To serve; spoon mac and cheese on plate, top with stir-fried beef and broccoli and garnish with sesame seeds.

Open sesame - let's eat!

Noodle Notes: ....

....

....

....

....

....

....

....

....

....

....

Szechuan Chicken Mac & Cheese

From thought to pot to plate: 45 minutes
Serves: 2

Ingredients:

your favorite box of mac & cheese	2 chicken breasts, in bite-sized pieces
1 cup of chicken broth	2 teaspoons of peanut oil
2 tablespoons of soy sauce	1 tablespoon of oyster sauce
1 tablespoon of white vinegar	3 cloves of garlic, minced
1 cup of carrots, peeled, chopped	1 teaspoon of red pepper flakes
¼ cup of fresh cilantro, chopped	¼ teaspoon of sesame oil
1 cup of broccoli florets	½ cup of frozen peas, thawed
3 green onions, sliced	

Cook mac & cheese as directed on the box. Combine the soy sauce, oyster sauce and white vinegar in a bowl and set aside. Heat peanut oil in wok over medium-high heat and add the chicken and garlic, followed by the carrots, broccoli, peas, green onion and red pepper flakes. Add the soy sauce mixture and stir to coat the chicken and vegetables. Simmer for about 3 minutes and stir in the sesame oil. Serve garnished with cilantro on a bed of mac & cheese.

Look at you! An international chef!

Forbidden City Mac & Cheese

From thought to pot to plate: 45 minutes

Serves: 4

Ingredients:

your favorite box of mac & cheese	4 chicken breasts, in bite-sized pieces
2 cups of fresh mushrooms, sliced	1 teaspoon of soy sauce
1 can of cream of celery soup	½ cup of water
1 can of water chestnuts, drained	1 cup of frozen peas, thawed
2 cups of mozzarella cheese, grated	dash of olive oil
salt and pepper to taste	1/2 cup of bamboo shoots

Preheat oven to 350°F. Cook mac & cheese as directed on the box. Cook the chicken in a heated pan with olive oil and soy sauce until browned. Combine the mac & cheese, chicken, mushrooms, water chestnuts and peas in a greased casserole dish. Mix together the soup with ½ cup of water chestnuts, bamboo shoots and peas and pour over the chicken, vegetable and mac & cheese mixture. Top with the cheese and bake for about 15 minutes or until bubbling and the top is golden brown. Let stand for 10 minutes before serving.

Enjoy!

Noodle Notes: ....

....

....

....

....

....

....

....

....

Cran Orange Chicken Mac & Cheese

From thought to pot to plate: 35 minutes
Serves: 4

Ingredients:

your favorite box of mac & cheese	3 chicken breasts, in bite-sized pieces
1 can of cream of chicken soup	1 package of stuffing mix
2 cups of mixed frozen vegetables	1 cup of orange juice
½ cup of dried cranberries	2 tbsp. of walnuts, chopped
dash of olive oil	

Preheat oven to 375°F. Cook mac & cheese as directed on the box. Prepare stuffing mix as directed on the package; but substitute orange juice for water and stir in the cranberries and walnuts. Set aside. Cook the chicken in a skillet with olive oil, and then add the soup and vegetables. Spoon the mac & cheese into a greased casserole dish, add then the chicken and top with stuffing. Bake for 20 minutes to heat through.

Enjoy!

Mac & Cheese Rice Bowl

From thought to pot to plate: 45 minutes
Serves: 4

Ingredients:

your favorite box of mac & cheese	1 cup of rice, uncooked
1 cup of frozen corn niblets, thawed	1 cup of frozen peas, thawed
1 teaspoon of soy sauce	1 teaspoon of butter

Cook all of the ingredients, with the exception of the mac & cheese, mixed together in a rice cooker, or bring to a boil on the stove. Cook mac & cheese as directed on the box. Once the mac & cheese and the rice mixture are ready, combine the two in a large bowl with soy sauce.

Bump up the carb load - tastes even better with bread!

Mac & Cheese Nasi Goreng

From thought to pot to plate: 40 minutes
Serves: 2

Ingredients:

your favorite box of mac & cheese	2 chicken breasts, in bite-sized pieces
1 cup of shrimp, peeled and deveined	5 red Thai chilies, diced
3 cloves of garlic, minced	½ teaspoon of shrimp paste
salt and pepper to taste	½ teaspoon of white sugar
½ tablespoon of soy sauce	1 tablespoon of cooking oil
½ cup of shallots, diced	2 leeks, finely chopped
3 stalks of celery, chopped	3 eggs, beaten
½ cup of white onion, diced	1 teaspoon of sambal oeleck
½ cup of frozen peas, thawed	½ cup of cucumber, chopped
¼ cup of roasted, unsalted peanuts	

Cook mac & cheese as directed on the box. Place chilies, garlic, shallots, salt, sugar and shrimp paste in a mortar and pestle and form a paste. In a skillet cook the beaten eggs omelet style. Remove from heat, chop and set aside. Heat the cooking oil in a wok until smoky. Add the paste and stir-fry for about a minute until the color turns brown. Add the chicken and soy sauce, sambal oeleck, peas, celery and leek and cook for another 4 minutes, then add the shrimp. Combine everything with the egg and served garnished with peanuts and cucumber on a bed of mac & cheese.

Enjoy!

Mac & Cheese California Roll

From thought to pot to plate: 45 minutes

Serves: 4

Ingredients:

your favorite box of mac & cheese	¼ cup of mayonnaise
½ cup of pollock (imitation crabmeat)	8 sheets of nori (edible seaweed)
2 tbsp. of toasted sesame seeds	2 avocados, sliced lengthwise
1 teaspoon of salt	1 cucumber, peeled, cut in thin strips
wasabi paste	soy sauce
pickled ginger	

Cook mac & cheese as directed on the box. Set in refrigerator to cool. Mix imitation crabmeat with mayonnaise in a bowl and set aside. To roll the sushi, cover a bamboo-rolling mat with plastic wrap. Lay a sheet of nori, shiny side down, on the wrap. Firmly pat down a thin, even layer of mac & cheese, leaving ¼" uncovered at the bottom edge of the sheet. Place 3 thinly sliced cucumber strips, 2 slices of avocado and about one tablespoon of the crab mixture in a line across the mac & cheese, about ¼" from the uncovered edge. Pick up the edge of the bamboo rolling sheet, fold the bottom edge of the sheet up enclosing the filling and tightly roll the sushi into a cylinder about 1½" in diameter. Once the sushi is rolled, wrap it in the mat and gently squeeze to compact it. Cut each roll into 1" pieces with a sharp knife dipped in water. Serve with soy sauce, wasabi and pickled ginger.

East meets West! Pasta meets rice! Macanori!

Mumbai Okra Mac & Cheese

From thought to pot to plate: 40 minutes
Serves: 2

Ingredients:

your favorite box of mac & cheese	¼ cup of butter
½ cup of white onion, diced	1lb. of fresh okra, sliced
½ teaspoon of ground cumin	½ teaspoon of fresh ginger, grated
½ teaspoon of ground coriander	salt and pepper to taste

Cook mac & cheese as directed on the box. In a large skillet and melt the butter on medium heat and add onion and sauté until tender. Stir in okra and add cumin, ginger, coriander and a little salt and pepper. Stir for a minute and then cover and let cook on low for 20 minutes or until tender. Serve the mac & cheese on the side of your okra.

This is dehlicious! If you're smart, don't invite your friends over for this... keep it to yourself!

Noodle Notes: ....
....
....
....
....
....
....
....
....
....
....
....
....
....

Madras Mac & Cheese

From thought to pot to plate: 45 minutes
Serves: 2

Ingredients:

your favorite box of mac & cheese	2 cups of frozen vegetables, thawed
1 can of garbanzo beans, drained	1 small cauliflower, cut into florets
½ cup of white onion, diced	3 cloves of garlic, minced
1 jar of madras curry sauce	

Preheat oven to 350°F. Cook mac & cheese as directed on the box. In an ovenproof bowl, combine the vegetables, garbanzo beans, cauliflower, onion, garlic and madras sauce. Bake covered in the oven until bubbling, approximately 35 minutes. Serve on a bed of mac & cheese.

Enjoy!

Oriental Mac & Cheese with Tuna

From thought to pot to plate: 25 minutes
Serves: 2

Ingredients:

your favorite box and mac & cheese	1 can of tuna, drained
1 cup of frozen peas, thawed	1 tablespoon of soy sauce
½ cup of water chestnuts, drained	½ cup of canned bamboo shoots, drained
salt and pepper to taste	½ cup of crunchy chow mien noodles

Cook mac & cheese as directed on the box. Mix in the can of tuna. Add peas, soy sauce, water chestnuts and bamboo shoots. Salt and pepper to taste. Top with crunchy chow mien noodles.

Grab your rickshaw and let's go!

Mac & Cheese Heads South

Mac & Cheese Jambalaya

From thought to pot to plate: 55 minutes

Serves: 4

Ingredients:

your favorite box of mac & cheese	2 chicken breasts, in bite-sized pieces
4 Andouille sausages, in ¼" slices	1lb. of shrimp, peeled and deveined
1 teaspoon of butter	1 cup of white onion, diced
2 teaspoons of paprika	1 teaspoon of cumin
1 teaspoon of cayenne pepper	½ cup of tomatoes, diced
1 green pepper, seeded and diced	2 stalks of celery, chopped
2 cups of chicken stock	4 green onions, sliced
2 cloves of garlic, minced	juice of one lemon
2 teaspoons of dried parsley	2 teaspoons of Cajun seasoning
½ teaspoon of dried thyme	salt and pepper to taste

Cook mac & cheese as directed on the box. Place butter and sausage in a large stockpot over medium heat, cook and stir for 5 minutes. Stir in all the spices and herbs and cook for another minute, followed by the tomatoes, garlic, onions, celery, green pepper, salt and pepper. Stir in chicken and chicken stock and turn heat to low. Cover and cook for about 40 minutes; and then lemon juice and shrimp and cook for another 5 minutes. Serve on a bed of mac & cheese, garnished with green onions.

Enjoy!

Bayou Shrimp Po' Boy Mac & Cheese

From thought to pot to plate: 40 minutes
Serves: 4

Ingredients:

your favorite box of mac & cheese	1lb. of shrimp, peeled and deveined
2 cups of red cabbage, finely shredded	2 tablespoons of relish
2 tablespoons of plain yogurt	1 teaspoon of mayonnaise
1 teaspoon of chili powder	½ teaspoon of paprika
salt and pepper to taste	¼ cup of red onion, diced
4 large buns	dash of olive oil

Cook mac & cheese as directed on the box. In a bowl, Stir together cabbage, relish, yogurt and mayo; set aside. Toss the shrimp with the olive oil, chili powder, paprika, salt and pepper together in a separate bowl. Over medium heat, cook the spiced shrimp until opaque. Toast the buns, and then spread the cabbage mixture on each side and top with red onion, a spoonful of mac & cheese and even portions of shrimp.

Enjoy!

Noodle Notes: ....

....

....

....

....

....

....

....

....

....

....

Crab Creamed Spinach Mac & Cheese

From thought to pot to plate: 45 minutes

Serves: 2

Ingredients:

your favorite box of mac & cheese	1 can of crabmeat, drained
1 box of frozen spinach, chopped	¼ cup of flour
1½ cups of cream	salt and pepper to taste
1 large egg, 2 large egg yolks	3 tablespoons of butter
2 cloves of garlic, minced	½ teaspoon of nutmeg
½ cup of white onion, diced	

Cook mac & cheese as directed on the box. Melt butter on medium heat in a saucepan. Add flour and whisk for approximately one minute until smooth. Take off heat and gradually add cream, salt and nutmeg. Place back on heat, whisk in the garlic and onion, and let mixture come to a boil; take off heat and stir to cool. In a big skillet on medium heat, add spinach and a dash of salt; cover and cook for about three minutes. Stir and continue to cook for another two minutes. Drain and cool slightly, squeeze spinach dry and chop. Put cream sauce back on the heat and add the eggs, mixing until sauce thickens. Add the crabmeat, pepper and the chopped spinach. Serve on a bed of mac & cheese.

Enjoy!

Honey Pecan Chicken Mac & Cheese

From thought to pot to plate: 40 minutes
Serves: 2

Ingredients:

your favorite box of mac & cheese	2 chicken breasts
1 teaspoon of dried thyme	½ teaspoons of curry powder
salt and pepper to taste	½ cup of liquid honey, warmed
2 teaspoons of grainy mustard	2 cloves of garlic, diced
1 cup of pecans, finely chopped	1 tablespoon of parsley, chopped

Preheat oven to oven to 375°F. Cook mac & cheese as directed on the box. Coat the chicken with the thyme, curry powder, salt and pepper in a shallow dish. Stir together the honey, mustard and garlic and pour over the chicken. Cover and chill for about 25 minutes. Remove from marinade and dredge chicken in pecans, placed in a shallow bowl. Bake chicken on a lightly greased sheet pan for approximately 35 minutes, or until cooked through. Serve on a bed of mac & cheese, garnished with parsley.

Enjoy!

Hey Macarena Mac & Cheese

From thought to pot to plate: 15 minutes
Serves: 2

Ingredients:

your favorite box of mac & cheese	generous helping of sass
cowboy boots	

Cook mac & cheese as directed on the box.

Serve with cocktail. Shake some booty.

New Orleans Blues Mac & Cheese

From thought to pot to plate: 45 minutes
Serves: 2

Ingredients:

your favorite box of mac & cheese	2 tablespoons of mesquite BBQ cheese
1 teaspoon of white vinegar	½ cup of Cheddar cheese, grated

Preheat oven to 350°F. Cook mac & cheese as directed on the box. Combine mac & cheese with BBQ sauce and vinegar in a casserole dish. Top with Cheddar and bake for about 15 minutes or until bubbling and the top is golden brown. Let stand for 10 minutes before serving.

Enjoy!

Mac & Cheese with Andouille Sausage

From thought to pot to plate: 45 minutes
Serves: 2

Ingredients:

your favorite box of mac & cheese	2 cups of Andouille sausage, sliced
2 red peppers, chopped	6 green onions, sliced
3 cloves of garlic, minced	½ cup of white onion, diced
2 teaspoons of Cajun seasoning	½ cup of Cheddar cheese, grated
dash of olive oil	

Preheat oven to 350°F. Cook mac & cheese as directed on the box. Cook the sausage with the red pepper, green onion, white onion and garlic until soft. Add Cajun seasoning and stir to combine. In a casserole dish combine the mac & cheese with the other ingredients and top with Cheddar cheese. Bake for about 15 minutes or until bubbling and the top is golden brown. Let stand for 10 minutes before serving.

Enjoy!

Fried Green Tomatoes Mac & Cheese

From thought to pot to plate: 45 minutes
Serves: 2

Ingredients:

your favorite box of mac & cheese	2 large green tomatoes, sliced
salt and pepper to taste	dash of white sugar
¼ cup of flour	2 eggs, beaten
1/3 cup Parmesan cheese, grated	2/3 cup of panko breadcrumbs
1/3 cup of olive oil	

Cook mac & cheese as directed on the box. Cut tomatoes into 1/3" thick slices and place on a sheet of foil. Sprinkle each with salt, pepper and a pinch of sugar and let stand for 15 minutes. Put flour, salt and pepper in a shallow bowl or pie plate. Pour beaten eggs into a second shallow bowl or pie plate. Mix panko and Parmesan together into the third plate or bowl. Heat olive oil in a large, non-stick pan, then dredge the tomato slices in the flour mixture and shake off the excess. Dip into eggs, then dredge in panko crumbs mixture. Cook coated tomato slices in hot oil until brown and crispy, about 3 to 5 minutes per side and drain on paper towels. Serve fried green tomatoes on top of your mac & cheese.

Quit your sass – get cookin'!

Noodle Notes: ....

....

....

....

....

....

....

....

....

Frontier
Mac & Cheese

Blazin' Saddles Mac & Cheese

From thought to pot to plate: 35 minutes
Serves: 4

Ingredients:

your favorite box of mac & cheese	1lb. of lean ground beef
package of taco seasoning mix (35 g.)	salt and pepper to taste
2 teaspoons of chili powder	1 jalapeno pepper, seeded and diced
1 can of green chiles, drained	2 cloves of garlic, minced
½ cup of red onion, diced	3 green onions, sliced
1 cup of Oaxaca cheese, grated	½ cup of fresh cilantro, chopped
juice and zest of one lime	2 Chipotle peppers, chopped
dash of hot sauce	dash of olive oil

Preheat oven to 350°F. Cook mac & cheese as directed on the box. In a skillet heat olive oil and cook the red onion and garlic until soft. Remove from the pan and then cook the ground beef until brown, adding the taco seasoning - prepared as directed on the package. Combine the mac & cheese, salt, pepper, seasoned beef, onions, garlic, chiles, cilantro, lime zest and juice, Chipotle peppers and hot sauce in a casserole dish. Top with Oaxaca cheese and bake for about 15 minutes or until bubbling and the top is golden brown. Let stand for 10 minutes before serving with a side of sour cream.

Yippee ki yay! Pass the water canteen!

Burrito Pie in the Sky Mac & Cheese

From thought to pot to plate: 45 minutes

Serves: 4

Ingredients:

2 boxes of your favorite mac & cheese	2lb. of lean ground beef
1 cup of white onion, diced	package of taco seasoning mix (35 g.)
1 teaspoon of chili powder	3 cloves of garlic, minced
1 can of sliced black olives, drained	1 can of green chiles, drained
1 can of refried beans	1 can of enchilada sauce
12 - 8" corn tortillas	1 cup of Monterey Jack cheese, grated
2 large tomatoes, chopped	salt and pepper to taste

Preheat oven to 350°F. Cook mac & cheese as directed on the box. Sauté meat in a skillet for 5 minutes, and add onion, garlic and taco seasoning prepared as directed on the package, stirring for another five minutes. Mix in the olives, chiles, tomatoes and refried beans. Reduce heat to low and simmer for about 20 minutes. Spread meat mixture in a large casserole dish and cover with the corn tortillas, followed by a layer of mac & cheese, then enchilada sauce topped with Monterey Jack cheese. Bake for about 20 minutes or until bubbling and the top is golden brown. Let stand for 10 minutes before serving.

The sky's the limit with mac & cheese!

Fiesta Mac & Cheese Bake

From thought to pot to plate: 30 minutes
Serves: 2

Ingredients:

your favorite box of mac & cheese	2 chicken breasts, in bite-sized pieces
1 can of green chiles, diced	2 cups of frozen corn, thawed
½ cup of white onion, diced	1 can of black beans, drained
1 cup of Cheddar cheese, grated	1 cup of fresh cilantro, chopped
2 stalks of celery, chopped	dash of olive oil
1 teaspoon of red pepper flakes	

Preheat oven to 375°F. Cook mac & cheese as directed on the box. Heat oil in skillet over medium heat, add chicken and brown; stir in chilies, corn, onions, beans, celery and cilantro. Cook for 3-4 minutes more. Pour mixture, along with the rinsed beans, in a casserole dish, layer on mac & cheese and top with Cheddar. Bake for about 15 minutes or until bubbling and the top is golden brown. Let stand for 10 minutes before serving.

Enjoy!

Noodle Notes: ....
....
....
....
....
....
....
....
....
....
....

Mac & Cheese Quesadillas

From thought to pot to plate: 45 minutes
Serves: 4

Ingredients:

your favorite box of mac & cheese	2 chicken breasts, in bite-sized pieces
½ cup of white onion, diced	3 cloves of garlic, minced
2 red peppers, chopped	dash of olive oil
½ cup of cilantro, chopped	1 cup of Cheddar cheese, grated
juice of one lemon	1 teaspoon of cayenne pepper
8 – 12" tortilla shells	½ cup of salsa
½ cup of sour cream	2 avocados, sliced

Cook mac & cheese as directed on the box. In a large skillet, heat oil over medium to high heat and cook chicken; add onions, garlic, cilantro, lemon juice and cayenne. Continue to cook for another 3 minutes. Lay 4 tortillas on work surface, spread each one with ¼ of the chicken mixture, then spread a layer of mac & cheese and grated cheese. Top each with another tortilla, pressing down to flatten. Heat on each side until lightly browned and cheese melted. Once all four are cooked, cut into wedges and serve with avocado, salsa and sour cream.

Delicioso!

Mac & Cheese Taco Salad Olé!

From thought to pot to plate: 25 minutes

Serves: 4

Ingredients:

your favorite box of mac & cheese	4 - 12" flour tortillas*
1lb. of lean ground beef	package of taco seasoning mix (35 g.)
1 can of black beans, drained	2 cloves of garlic, minced
½ head of iceberg lettuce, shredded	2 cups of Cheddar cheese, grated
1 cup of tomatoes, chopped	3 green onions, sliced
½ cup of salsa	½ cup of sour cream

Cook mac & cheese as directed on the box. Set aside to cool. In a large skillet brown the ground beef and garlic with the taco seasoning as directed on the package. Layer the lettuce, mac & cheese, rinsed beans, tomatoes and beef, and top with Cheddar, salsa, sour cream and green onion in taco bowls.

* Use flour tortillas to make the taco bowls. Preheat oven to 400°F. Place 4 mason jars upside down, spaced evenly on a sheet pan (or use an upside down muffin tin and nestle tortillas between the muffin portions). Microwave the tortillas for 20 seconds to soften them. Brush them with a little canola oil and drape over jars. Bake the tortillas for about 8 minutes, until crisped and brown. Let cool for a few minutes before removing.

Practically diet food!

Mexican Chorizo Mac & Cheese

From thought to pot to plate: 45 minutes
Serves: 2

Ingredients:

your favorite box of mac & cheese	dash of olive oil
4 Mexican chorizo sausages	½ cup of white onion, diced
1 red pepper, seeded and diced	2 jalapenos, diced
1 cup of Tex-Mex cheese, grated	1 cup of corn niblets, thawed
1 can of black beans, drained	juice of one lemon
½ cup of panko breadcrumbs	

Preheat oven to 375°F. Cook mac & cheese as directed on the box. Cook the sausage (casing removed) in a large skillet on medium heat until dry and crisp – about two minutes. Add the red onion, red pepper and jalapenos and cook until onions are soft. Stir in the corn, rinsed black beans and lime juice, and combine all of the ingredients with the mac & cheese in a greased casserole dish, topped evenly with panko. Bake for about 15 minutes or until bubbling and the top is golden brown. Let stand for 10 minutes before serving.

Enjoy!

Sombrero Mac & Cheese

From thought to pot to plate: 30 minutes
Serves: 2

Ingredients:

your favorite box of mac & cheese	1 can of prepared chili
½ cup of Cheddar cheese, grated	2 jalapeno peppers, diced

Cook mac & cheese as directed on the box. Heat the chili and add to the mac & cheese, stir together. Top with grated Cheddar and chopped jalapenos.

Fantastico!

Mexico City Mac & Cheese Lasagna

From thought to pot to plate: 50 minutes

Serves: 4

Ingredients:

2 boxes of your favorite mac & cheese	2lb. of lean ground beef
1 cup of white onion, diced	1 can of sliced black olives, drained
1½ cup of pepper jack cheese, grated	1 cup of salsa
2 cans of green chiles, drained	

Preheat oven to 350°F. Cook mac & cheese as directed on the box. Brown the beef and onions in a skillet; then add the green chiles and olives. Remove from the heat once cooked. Spread one half of the meat mixture in a greased casserole dish. Top with half of the mac & cheese and spoon a ½ cup of salsa on top. Repeat the meat, mac & cheese and salsa layers and top with the pepper jack cheese. Bake for about 25 minutes or until bubbling and the top is golden brown. Let stand for 10 minutes before serving.

Don't tell anyone you are making this… people will be jealous!

Noodle Notes: ....

....

....

....

....

....

....

....

....

....

....

....

Taos Chicken Mac & Cheese

From thought to pot to plate: 35 minutes

Serves: 4

Ingredients:

your favorite box of mac & cheese	3 chicken breasts, in bite-sized pieces
1 can of black beans, drained	1 yellow pepper, chopped
1 can of cream of chicken soup	½ cup of water
¼ cup of fresh cilantro, chopped	1 jalapeno pepper, diced
1 cup of salsa verde	1 cup of Tex-Mex cheese, grated
salt and pepper to taste	dash of olive oil

Preheat oven to 350°F. Cook mac & cheese as directed on the box. In a heated skillet, cook the chicken with the yellow pepper and jalapeno in olive oil. Combine the mac & cheese, cilantro, salsa verde and chicken mixture with a combination of the cream of chicken soup and water in a casserole dish. Top with cheese and bake for about 20 minutes or until bubbling and the top is golden brown. Let stand for 10 minutes before serving.

Enjoy!

Noodle Notes: ....

....

....

....

....

....

....

....

....

....

174

Tex-Mex Mac & Cheese

From thought to pot to plate: 40 minutes

Serves: 2

Ingredients:

your favorite box of mac & cheese	1 cup of Tex-Mex cheese, grated
4 green chiles, chopped	1 cup of salsa
3 green onions, sliced	1 teaspoon of cumin
1 teaspoon of paprika	1 cup of black beans, drained
1 tablespoon of fresh cilantro, chopped	1 avocado, sliced

Preheat oven to 350°F. Cook mac & cheese as directed on the box. Combine the mac & cheese, chiles, salsa, onions, spices and rinsed black beans in a large casserole dish. Top with Tex-Mex cheese and bake for 20 minutes or until bubbling and the top is golden brown. Serve topped with cilantro and sliced avocado.

Enjoy!

Noodle Notes:

....

....

....

....

....

....

....

....

....

....

....

....

....

Hoedown Mac & Cheese

From thought to pot to plate: 35 minutes

Serves: 4

Ingredients:

your favorite box of mac & cheese	2 chicken breasts, cut into strips
1 red pepper, chopped	2 cups of frozen corn niblets, thawed
1 fresh jalapeno pepper, diced	salt and pepper to taste
dash of hot sauce	½ cup of red cabbage, thinly sliced
¼ cup of flour	2 eggs, beaten
¼ cup of canola oil	1 tablespoon of fresh cilantro, chopped

Cook mac & cheese as directed on the box. Coat the chicken pieces with egg, then in a small bowl combine the flour, salt and pepper and dredge the chicken pieces until coated. Once coated, cook in hot oil. Combine the crispy chicken with the corn, red jalapeno, cilantro, hot sauce and red cabbage and serve on a bed of mac & cheese.

Hee haw that's good!

Noodle Notes: ....
....
....
....
....
....
....
....
....
....
....

176

Mac & Cheese Baja Taco

From thought to pot to plate: 45 minutes

Serves: 4

Ingredients:

your favorite box of mac & cheese	2 tilapia fillets
package of taco seasoning mix (35 g.)	¼ cup of white cabbage, shredded
¼ cup of red cabbage, shredded	¼ teaspoon of celery salt
1 teaspoon of white vinegar	2 green onions, sliced
1 teaspoon of mayonnaise	½ carrot, shredded
1 cup of fresh cilantro, chopped	1 tablespoon of butter
1 cup of salsa	12 - 6" corn tortillas
1 lemon, cut into wedges	dash of hot sauce

Cook mac & cheese as directed on the box. Combine the red and white cabbage, carrot, green onion, celery salt, mayonnaise, vinegar and half of the cilantro in a bowl. Coat the tilapia with the taco seasoning and in a skillet cook the coated fish in butter, turning once until golden brown. Lay out the tortillas on a large serving tray. Put a spoonful of mac & cheese on each, following by some fish and the coleslaw mixture. Garnish with the remaining cilantro, hot sauce and lemon wedges. Serve with guacamole.

If you don't want to share this meal, don't tell anyone you are making it and don't answer your door!

Chipotle and Onion Mac & Cheese

From thought to pot to plate: 45 minutes

Serves: 2

Ingredients:

your favorite box of mac & cheese	dash of olive oil
1 tablespoon of butter	1 large white onion, thinly sliced
2 cloves of garlic, minced	1 tablespoon of sugar
½ Chipotle pepper, diced	1 cup of Tex-Mex cheese, grated
salt and pepper to taste	

Preheat oven to 375°F. Cook mac & cheese as directed on the box. Heat oil and butter in large skillet over medium heat; add onions and sauté until tender. Add the sugar and turn heat down - cook for about 20 minutes until golden brown, then add the garlic and Chipotle and cook for another minute. Combine the onions, garlic and Chipotle with the mac & cheese with salt and pepper in a casserole dish and top with Tex-Mex cheese. Bake for about 20 minutes or until bubbling and the top is golden brown. Let stand for 10 minutes before serving.

Enjoy!

Noodle Notes: ....

....

....

....

....

....

....

....

....

....

Corn and Green Chile Mac & Cheese

From thought to pot to plate: 40 minutes

Serves: 2

Ingredients:

your favorite box of mac & cheese	½ cup of white onion, diced
1 cup of frozen corn, thawed	2 cans of green chiles, chopped
½ teaspoon of cayenne pepper	salt and pepper to taste
½ cup of panko breadcrumbs	½ cup of Monterey Jack cheese, grated
½ cup of white Cheddar cheese, grated	dash of olive oil

Preheat oven to 350°F. Cook mac & cheese as directed on the box. In a skillet on medium heat sauté the onion in olive oil until soft. Combine the mac & cheese, salt, pepper, corn, drained chiles, onion, Monterey Jack cheese and cayenne pepper in a casserole dish and top with the Cheddar cheese and panko. Bake for about 15 minutes or until bubbling and the top is golden brown. Let stand for 10 minutes before serving.

Enjoy!

Campfire Mac & Cheese

From thought to pot to plate: 30 minutes

Serves: 2

Ingredients:

your favorite box of mac & cheese	2 wieners
2 tablespoons of ketchup	1 cup of Cheddar cheese, grated
salt and pepper to taste	

Cook mac & cheese as directed on the box. Cook wieners on open flame and when cooked, slice into bite-sized pieces. Combine the mac & cheese, Cheddar, sliced wieners, salt, pepper and ketchup in a skillet and cook on open flame until bubbling.

Don't forget the marshmallows for dessert!

Buffalo Chicken Mac & Cheese

From thought to pot to plate: 40 minutes

Serves: 2

Ingredients:

your favorite box of mac & cheese	2 chicken breasts, in bite-sized pieces
1 cup of red onion, diced	3 stalks of celery, chopped
2 clove of garlic, minced	1/4 cup of hot sauce
2 tablespoons of butter	2 tablespoons of flour
2 teaspoons of dry mustard	2½ cups of half and half cream
½ cup of Tex-Mex cheese, grated	½ cup of sour cream
1 cup of breadcrumbs	3 tablespoons of chopped parsley
½ cup of blue cheese, crumbled	salt and pepper to taste

Preheat oven to 350°F. Cook mac & cheese as directed on the box. Melt a tablespoon of butter in a large skillet and cook the chicken, onion, garlic and celery over medium heat. Add the hot sauce and continue to simmer. In a saucepan, melt the other table-spoon of butter together with the flour and mustard to make a roux, then whisk in the half and half and stir until thick, followed by the Tex-Mex and blue cheese, salt and pepper, sour cream and parsley. Combine the chicken, cheese mix and mac & cheese in a greased casserole dish and top with breadcrumbs. Bake for about 20 minutes or until bubbling and the top is golden brown. Let stand for 10 minutes before serving.

Enjoy!

Chiapas Mac & Cheese

From thought to pot to plate: 40 minutes
Serves: 2

Ingredients:

your favorite box of mac & cheese	4 Mexican chorizo sausages, sliced
1 cup of Monterey Jack cheese, grated	2 red peppers, diced
½ cup of fresh cilantro, chopped	6 green onions, sliced
2 fresh jalapenos, diced	1 cup of frozen corn, thawed
2 cloves of garlic, minced	½ cup of red onion, diced

Preheat oven to 375°F. Cook mac & cheese as directed on the box. Cook sliced chorizo in a medium skillet, then remove from heat and place on a paper towel to drain. Place the red peppers, corn, green onion, red onion, garlic and jalapenos in the skillet and cook until soft. Combine the peppers mixture with most of the cilantro, chorizo and mac & cheese and put in a greased casserole dish, topped with Monterey Jack cheese. Bake for 25 minutes or until bubbling and the top is golden brown. Let stand for ten minutes before serving, and sprinkle remaining cilantro on top.

Dos cervasas por favor señor.

Noodle Notes: ....
....
....
....
....
....
....
....
....
....

Mac & Cheese Double B Enchiladas

From thought to pot to plate: 45 minutes

Serves: 4

Ingredients:

your favorite box of mac & cheese	1lb. of lean ground beef
½ cup of white onion, diced	1 teaspoon of chili powder
2 green chiles, seeded and diced	1 teaspoon of ground cumin
1 can of pinto beans, drained	1 cup of sour cream
¼ teaspoon of garlic powder	12 - 6" corn tortillas
1 can of enchilada sauce	1 cup of Cheddar cheese, grated

Preheat oven to 375°F. Cook mac & cheese as directed on the box. In a large skillet cook the ground beef, chilies, cumin and onion. Stir the rinsed pinto beans into the meat mixture and set aside. In a small mixing bowl, combine the sour cream and garlic powder. Cut tortillas in half and place enough to cover the bottom of a greased 9" x 13" casserole dish. Top with half of the meat mixture, then half of the sour cream mixture, a layer of mac & cheese and half of the enchilada sauce. Repeat layers. Cover dish and chill in the refrigerator overnight. When ready to cook, replace the wrap with foil and bake for 35 to 40 minutes at 350°F until bubbling. Uncover, top with cheese and bake for 5 minutes longer.

"So, this enchilada walks into a bar... "

Mac & Cheese Fiesta Tacos

From thought to pot to plate: 35 minutes
Serves: 4

Ingredients:

your favorite box of mac & cheese	1lb. of lean ground beef
package of taco seasoning mix (35 g.)	¾ cup of water
½ cup of white onion, diced	2 tomatoes, diced
1 clove of garlic, minced	½ head of iceberg lettuce, chopped
3 green onions, sliced	2 jalapenos, diced
1½ cups of Tex-Mex cheese, grated	hot sauce
12 taco shells	1 cup of salsa
1 cup of sour cream	

Preheat oven to 250°F to warm the tacos. Cook mac & cheese as directed on the box. In a large skillet, cook meat until brown, stirring in the taco seasoning prepared as directed on the package. Once cooked, set the meat aside. Cook the onion and garlic until soft, and then combine with the meat. In small bowls assemble the meat, mac & cheese, tomatoes, hot sauce, salsa, sour cream, cheese, green onion, jalapenos and lettuce separately for everyone to fill their own warmed tacos.

Where's my sombrero? Olé!

Hatch Chile Mac & Cheese

From thought to pot to plate: 35 minutes

Serves: 2

Ingredients:

your favorite box of mac & cheese	¾lb. of Hatch chiles, roasted, diced
½ teaspoon of cayenne pepper	dash of salt
½ teaspoon of dry mustard powder	½ cup of white onion, diced
3 cloves of garlic, minced	1 teaspoon of ground coriander
1 cup of breadcrumbs	salt and pepper to taste

Preheat oven to 350°F. Cook mac & cheese as directed on the box; add cayenne, salt and mustard and transfer to a casserole dish. Heat oil in skillet, add onion and garlic; sauté until tender and then add roasted and peeled chiles and coriander. Spread mixture over mac & cheese, top with crumbs and bake for 15 minutes or until heated through and golden brown.

Olé!

Noodle Notes: ....

....

....

....

....

....

....

....

....

....

....

....

Salsa Verde Chicken Mac & Cheese

From thought to pot to plate: 40 minutes
Serves: 2

Ingredients:

your favorite box of mac & cheese	2 chicken breasts, in bite-sized pieces
1 cup of white onion, diced	3 cloves of garlic, minced
1 cup of salsa verde	½ cup of fresh cilantro, chopped
1 tablespoon of fresh lemon juice	salt and pepper to taste
dash of olive oil	½ cup of Monterey Jack cheese, grated

Preheat oven to 350°F. Cook mac & cheese as directed on the box. In a large skillet, heat olive oil on medium heat and cook the chicken, then add the onion and garlic and sauté until soft. Combine the mac & cheese, chicken mixture, cilantro, lemon juice, salsa verde, salt and pepper in a casserole dish and top with Monterey Jack. Bake for about 20 minutes or until bubbling and the top is golden brown. Let stand for 10 minutes before serving.

Buenos días!

Noodle Notes: ....

....

....

....

....

....

....

....

....

....

....

....

Ride 'Em Cowboy Mac & Cheese Stew

From thought to pot to plate: 40 minutes
Serves: 2

Ingredients:

your favorite box of mac & cheese	2lbs. of sirloin steak, in bite-sized pieces
1lb. of ham hock, in bite-sized pieces	2 cans of pinto beans, drained
dash of olive oil	1 cup of white onion, diced
1 tablespoon of molasses	1 can of green chilies, diced
1 can of stewed tomatoes	1 can of tomato paste
dash of hot sauce	salt and pepper to taste
sourdough bread	

Cook mac & cheese as directed on the box. In a large stockpot, sauté the steak and onions. Add the ham hock and rinsed pinto beans. Let cook for about 3 minutes, and then add the stewed tomatoes, molasses, tomato paste and drained chiles. Season with hot sauce, salt and pepper and let simmer for about 25 minutes. Serve stew on a bed of mac & cheese with sourdough bread.

Just so you know, if you are eating cowboy food, you need to have it with coffee. That's a rule. A cowboy rule.

South of the Border Mac & Cheese

From thought to pot to plate: 35 minutes

Serves: 2

Ingredients:

your favorite box of mac & cheese	½ lb. of ground pork
1 cup of frozen corn, thawed	½ cup of white onion, diced
dash of olive oil	1 teaspoon of chili powder
1 teaspoon of paprika	1 teaspoon of cumin
2 cloves of garlic, minced	salt and pepper to taste
½ cup of pepper jack cheese, grated	½ cup of sour cream
jalapenos, for garnish	½ cup of fresh cilantro, chopped
½ cup of red onion, diced	

Preheat oven to 350°F. Cook mac & cheese as directed on the box. Place pork in a bowl and toss together with the spices and white onion. In a skillet cook the spiced pork until brown and onions soft; then combine with the corn and mac & cheese. Place mixture in a greased casserole dish and top with cheese. Bake for about 15 minutes or until bubbling and the top is golden brown. Serve with sides of red onion, sour cream, cilantro and jalapenos for garnish.

Noodle Notes: ....
....
....
....
....
....
....
....
....
....

Texas Caviar Mac & Cheese

From thought to pot to plate: 40 minutes

Serves: 4

Ingredients:

your favorite box of mac & cheese	1 can of black beans, drained
1 can of Mexicorn, drained	3 tomatoes, chopped
½ cup of red onion, diced	2 avocados, chopped
¼ cup of olive oil	1 tablespoon of red wine vinegar
package of taco seasoning mix (35 g.)	1 package of corn tortillas

Cook mac & cheese as directed on the box; set aside in the refrigerator to chill. Combine all of the other ingredients, with the exception of the chips. Stir to combine, along with the chilled mac & cheese. Serve with tortilla chips.

Enjoy!

Noodle Notes:

Tijuana Mac & Cheese Enchiladas

From thought to pot to plate: 45 minutes

Serves: 4

Ingredients:

your favorite box of mac & cheese	4 chicken breasts, in bite-sized pieces
1 large green pepper, chopped	1 large red pepper, chopped
1 large yellow pepper, chopped	1 tablespoon of chili powder
2 cups of salsa verde	1 package of cream cheese
1 cup of Tex-Mex cheese, grated	12 - 9" flour tortillas, warmed slightly
1 cup of fresh cilantro, chopped	

Preheat oven to 375°F. Cook mac & cheese as directed on the box. In a skillet cook the chicken and peppers. Add the chili powder and stir in cream cheese. In a large bowl, combine the chicken mixture with the mac & cheese and spoon it all into the center of each tortilla, roll and place in baking dish. Pour salsa verde on top of the rolls and sprinkle on grated cheese. Bake for about 15 minutes or until bubbling and the top is golden brown. Let stand for 10 minutes before serving and garnish with cilantro.

Enjoy!

Sufferin' Succotash Mac & Cheese

From thought to pot to plate: 35 minutes
Serves: 2

Ingredients:

box of mac & white Cheddar cheese	1 tablespoon of oil
1 cup of cooked ham, cubed	2 carrots, peeled, diced
½ cup red pepper, chopped	1 cup of frozen corn, thawed
3 green onions, sliced	1 cup frozen baby lima beans, thawed
salt and pepper to taste	

Cook mac & cheese as directed on the box. Heat oil in skillet over medium high heat. Sauté ham, carrots and red pepper, followed by the corn, green onions, lima beans, salt and pepper. Cover and take off heat, let stand for 2 minutes. Serve on a bed of mac & cheese.

Sylvester never had it so good!

Noodle Notes: ....
....
....
....
....
....
....
....
....
....
....
....

Oaxaca Mac & Cheese

From thought to pot to plate: 45 minutes
Serves: 2

Ingredients:

your favorite box of mac & cheese	2 teaspoons of Ancho chiles, diced
2 cloves of garlic, diced	1 cup of Oaxaca cheese, grated
dash of hot sauce	½ cup of panko breadcrumbs
1 tablespoon of butter	salt and pepper to taste

Preheat oven to 375°. Cook mac & cheese as directed on the box. Melt butter in a large saucepan and add the garlic, chiles, hot sauce, salt and pepper. Combine in a casserole dish with the mac & cheese along with the Oaxaca cheese. Cover with panko and bake for about 15 minutes or until bubbling and the top is golden brown. Let stand for 10 minutes before serving.

Enjoy!

Noodle Notes: ....
....
....
....
....
....
....
....
....
....
....
....
....
....

Mac & Cheese Black Bean Burritos

From thought to pot to plate: 45 minutes
Serves: 4

Ingredients:

your favorite box of mac & cheese	dash of olive oil
½ cup of white onion, diced	3 cloves of garlic, minced
1 jalapeno, seeded and diced	½ teaspoon of ground cumin
salt and pepper to taste	2 tablespoons of tomato paste
1 cup of frozen corn niblets, thawed	2 green onions, sliced
1 can of black beans, drained	1 cup of prepared salsa
juice of one lime	2 cups of Monterey Jack cheese, grated
1 cup of iceberg lettuce, shredded	½ cup of sour cream
2 avocados, sliced	1 lime, cut into wedges
8 - 12" flour tortillas	

Cook mac & cheese as directed on the box. Cook the onions and garlic in olive oil until soft, and then add the jalapeno, cumin, salt, pepper, tomato paste, corn, green onions and beans. Top each tortilla with the bean mixture, a spoonful of mac & cheese and roll together. Garnish burritos with cheese, sour cream, lettuce, avocado and a wedge of lime.

Enjoy!

Bandana Mac & Cheese

From thought to pot to plate: 45 minutes
Serves: 2

Ingredients:

your favorite box of mac & cheese	3 slices of bacon, chopped
1 chicken breast, in bite-sized pieces	2 tablespoons of Ranch dressing
½ cup of red onion, diced	½ cup of Monterey Jack cheese, grated
dash of olive oil	salt and pepper to taste

Preheat oven to 350°F. Cook mac & cheese as directed on the box. In a skillet, cook the bacon until crispy. Remove from pan and drain on a paper towel. Wipe the pan clean and cook the chicken and onion in olive oil. Combine the bacon, chicken, onion, mac & cheese, salt, pepper and ranch dressing in a greased casserole dish, sprinkle the top with Monterey Jack cheese and bake for about 15 minutes or until bubbling and the top is golden brown. Let stand for 10 minutes before serving.

Seriously? This rocks!

Noodle Notes: ....

....

....

....

....

....

....

....

....

....

....

....

Mac & Cheese Goes for a Dip

Mac & Cheese Crab Cakes

From thought to pot to plate: 50 minutes
Serves: 6

Ingredients:

your favorite box of mac & cheese	1lb. of crabmeat, drained
1¼ cups of breadcrumbs	¼ cup of red peppers, diced
3 green onions, sliced	1 tablespoon of fresh parsley, chopped
1 egg, beaten	2 teaspoons of mayonnaise
juice of one lemon	1 tablespoon of grainy mustard
1 teaspoon of Worcestershire sauce	dash of olive oil
salt and pepper to taste	¼ teaspoon of garlic powder
dash of cayenne pepper	¼ cup of cornmeal
1 tablespoon of butter	

Preheat oven to 350°F. Cook mac & cheese as directed on the box. In a large bowl combine the crabmeat, breadcrumbs, red pepper, green onion, garlic powder, cayenne pepper and parsley. In a second bowl combine the mayonnaise, egg, mustard, Worcestershire and lemon juice. Combine the wet and dry ingredients and refrigerate for about half an hour. Form the crab cakes and brown in melted butter in a hot skillet – for about 3 minutes a side. Carefully transfer the crab cakes to a sheet pan and place in the oven for 10 minutes or until heated through. Serve with a side of mac & cheese.

Enjoy!

Amalfi Coast Halibut with Mac & Cheese

From thought to pot to plate: 35 minutes

Serves: 4

Ingredients:

your favorite box of mac & cheese	4 small halibut fillets, deboned
1 can of diced tomatoes, not drained	¼ cup of vinaigrette
1 cup of arugula	1 cup of mozzarella, grated
one lemon, cut into wedges	

Preheat oven to 350°F. Cook mac & cheese as directed on the box. Place the halibut in a casserole dish, covered with the tomatoes and vinaigrette and sprinkle with mozzarella. Bake for about 25 minutes or until bubbling and the top is golden brown. Serve garnished with a handful of arugula and a lemon wedge on a bed of mac & cheese.

Enjoy!

NYC Style Mac & Cheese

From thought to pot to plate: 40 minutes

Serves: 2

Ingredients:

your favorite box of mac & cheese	1 small red onion, sliced in rings
1½ cup of gravlax	salt and pepper to taste
2 tablespoons of capers	1 tablespoon of fresh dill, chopped
1 package of cream cheese	1 lemon, cut into wedges

Cook the mac & cheese as directed on the box. Once cooked, spread over the bottom of a casserole dish and put in the refrigerator to chill. Once cold, spread the mac & cheese with a layer of cream cheese, then the gravlax, following by red onion rings, dill and capers. Garnish with lemon slices to be squeezed on each portion.

This is dedicated to my friend Sarah, who loves seafood and carbs.

Crabby Mac & Cheese

From thought to pot to plate: 40 minutes
Serves: 2

Ingredients:

your favorite box of mac & cheese	1 can of crabmeat, drained
1 tablespoon of butter	4 cloves garlic, minced
½ teaspoon of red pepper flakes	½ cup of half and half
2 teaspoons of mayonnaise	1 tablespoon of grainy mustard
½ cup of Gruyere cheese, grated	5 green onions, sliced
¾ cup panko breadcrumbs	¼ cup Parmesan cheese, grated
salt and pepper to taste	

Preheat oven to 350°F. Cook mac & cheese as directed on the box. Melt the butter in a pan and add the garlic and red pepper flakes and cook for about a minute, then add the flour and stir until golden brown. Add the cream and cook until it thickens – for about 5 minutes. Add the mayonnaise, mustard, salt and pepper; then mix in the Gruyere. Combine everything with the mac & cheese, crab and green onions. Place in a casserole dish and top with panko and Parmesan. Bake in the oven for about 20 minutes, or until bubbling and the top is golden brown.

Enjoy!

Goddess Mac & Cheese

From thought to pot to plate: 30 minutes

Serves: 2

Ingredients:

your favorite box of mac & cheese	1 anchovy, finely chopped
1 clove of garlic, minced	½ teaspoon of lime zest
3 tablespoons of parsley, chopped	1 tablespoon of fresh cilantro, chopped
2 tablespoon of fresh basil, chopped	2 shallots, diced
¼ teaspoon of grainy mustard	1 cup of mozzarella, grated
dash of olive oil	

Preheat oven to 350°F. Cook mac & cheese as directed on the box. Put garlic and anchovy in a small food processor and blend until a paste, or chop with a knife until minced. Add the olive oil, lime zest, parsley, cilantro, basil, shallots and mustard. Transfer to a larger bowl and combine with the mac & cheese and mozzarella.

Bake for about 15 minutes or until bubbling. Let stand for 10 minutes before serving.

For dishy goddesses everywhere!

Noodle Notes: ....
....
....
....
....
....
....
....
....
....

Lobster Mac & Cheese

From thought to pot to plate: 30 minutes
Serves: 2

Ingredients:

your favorite box of mac & cheese	1 can of lobster meat, chopped
dash of olive oil	½ cup of white onion, diced
1 clove of garlic, minced	2 shallots, diced
½ cup of fresh parsley, chopped	1 cup of Gruyere cheese, grated
½ cup of breadcrumbs	salt and pepper to taste

Preheat oven to 350°F. Cook mac & cheese as directed on the box. In a large skillet, sauté the onion, garlic and shallots in olive oil until soft. Place the mac & cheese in a bowl and fold in the lobster, Gruyere and sautéed vegetables. Transfer to a casserole dish and top with breadcrumbs and parsley. Bake for about 20 minutes or until bubbling and the top is golden brown. Let stand for 10 minutes before serving.

This recipe is also known as "Up Town Mac & Cheese."

Noodle Notes: ....

....

....

....

....

....

....

....

....

....

....

....

Mac & Cheese Shrimp Primavera

From thought to pot to plate: 40 minutes
Serves: 2

Ingredients:

your favorite box of mac & cheese	dash of olive oil
2 cups of shrimp, deveined	3 cloves of garlic, minced
½ cup of red onion, diced	½ cup of chicken broth
1 cup of frozen peas, thawed	1 bunch of spinach, chopped
½ cup of marinated artichoke hearts	1 tablespoon of lemon juice
1 teaspoon of dill	salt and pepper to taste

Cook mac & cheese as directed on the box. In a large skillet, sauté the shrimp, garlic and onion. Once shrimp are translucent and the onion and garlic soft; add chicken broth, peas and stemmed spinach and let simmer uncovered for 2 minutes more. Fold into mac & cheese with chopped artichoke hearts, dill and lemon juice. Season with salt and pepper and serve.

The food of mermaids!

Noodle Notes: ....

....

....

....

....

....

....

....

....

....

....

....

"Go To" Mac & Cheese

From thought to pot to plate: 40 minutes
Serves: 4

Ingredients:

your favorite box of mac & cheese	¼ cup of Italian Dressing
2 cans of tuna, drained	1 cup of Cheddar cheese, grated

Preheat oven to 375°F. Cook mac & cheese as directed. Stir in the dressing, tuna and ½ cup of Cheddar cheese. Mix well and pour into a casserole dish. Cover with foil and place in oven to bake for 25 minutes. Remove from oven, uncover, sprinkle the rest of the cheese and bake for about 10 minutes or until bubbling and the top is golden brown. Let stand for 5 minutes before serving.

For a balanced approach, try some vegetables or a salad on the side. See, we are trying!

Salmon Dill Mac & Cream Cheese

From thought to pot to plate: 45 minutes
Serves: 2

Ingredients:

your favorite box of mac & cheese	3 green onions, chopped
2 cloves of garlic, minced	dash of olive oil
salt and pepper to taste	2 tablespoons of fresh dill, chopped
1 cup of cream cheese	1½ cup of smoked salmon, bite-sized pieces

Cook mac & cheese as directed on the box. In a skillet, heat olive oil and cook green onion and garlic until soft; and then add salt, pepper and dill. Combine the mac & cheese, cream cheese, onion mixture and salmon together and serve.

Addie loves this dish, so will you!

Herby Shrimp Mac & Cheese

From thought to pot to plate: 35 minutes
Serves: 2

Ingredients:

your favorite box of mac & cheese	approx.. 30 shrimp, peeled, deveined
juice of two large lemons	1 cup of panko breadcrumbs
1 cup of fresh parsley, chopped	½ cup of red onion, diced
1 tablespoon of butter	salt and pepper to taste
1 tablespoon of fresh dill, chopped	1 cup of Gruyere cheese, grated

Cook mac & cheese as directed on the box. In a large skillet, melt the butter and sauté the onion until soft; add shrimp, dill, parsley, lemon juice, salt and pepper. In a greased casserole dish fold the shrimp mixture with mac & cheese and Gruyere, reserving a bit of cheese to sprinkle on top, along with the panko. Bake for 15 minutes or until bubbling and golden brown on top.

Enjoy!

Noodle Notes: ....

....

....

....

....

....

....

....

....

....

....

....

....

Luxury Fish Pie Mac & Cheese

From thought to pot to plate: 45 minutes

Serves: 4

Ingredients:

your favorite box of mac & cheese	2 teaspoons of capers
4 tilapia fillets, in bite-sized pieces	¼ cup of flour
2 tablespoons of fresh dill, chopped	1 egg, beaten
½ cup of crème fraiche	½ cup of half and half
dash of olive oil	4 cloves of garlic, minced
1 cup of white onion, diced	salt and pepper to taste
½ cup of Gruyere cheese, grated	1 teaspoon of butter
½ cup of panko crumbs	

Preheat oven to 350°F. Cook mac & cheese as directed on the box. In a large skillet, heat olive oil and sauté the garlic and onion. Remove and set aside. In a bowl, combine the salt, pepper and flour and dredge the pieces of tilapia in the mixture. Melt the butter in the skillet and place the coated pieces of fish in it, sautéing until cooked. Combine the onion mixture with the fish, crème fraiche, half and half, capers, chopped dill and the beaten egg with the mac & cheese and place in a large casserole dish. Top the dish with Gruyere and panko and bake for 30 minutes or until bubbling and heated through.

They don't call this luxury fish pie for nothing!

Mac & Cheese with Mussels

From thought to pot to plate: 35 minutes
Serves: 2

Ingredients:

your favorite box of mac & cheese	1lb. of fresh mussels
½ cup of white wine	4 cloves of garlic, minced
dash of red pepper flakes	2 tablespoons of parsley, chopped
dash of olive oil	1 green onion, sliced
1 lemon, sliced into wedges	

Cook mac & cheese as directed on the box. Scrub mussels under cold water and discard ones that do not open when tapped. In a large saucepan bring wine, garlic, green onion and red pepper flakes to a boil. Turn down the heat and add mussels, cover and cook covered until they are all open – about six minutes. Drain the mussels and serve still in the shell on a bed of mac & cheese, garnished with parsley and a few lemon wedges.

Enjoy!

Noodle Notes: ....

....

....

....

....

....

....

....

....

....

....

....

Ladies Who Lunch Mac & Cheese

From thought to pot to plate: 35 minutes
Serves: 2

Ingredients:

your favorite box of mac & cheese	1 can of salmon, drained
½ cup of red onion, diced	2 teaspoons of fresh dill, chopped
salt and pepper to taste	1 tablespoon of mayonnaise
2 cloves of garlic, minced	3 stalks of celery, chopped
juice of one lemon	dash of olive oil
½ cup of Cheddar cheese, grated	

Preheat oven to 350°F. Cook mac & cheese as directed on the box. In a skillet, cook the red onion, garlic and celery in olive oil until soft. Combine the mac & cheese, onion and celery mixture, lemon juice, fresh dill, salt, pepper, mayonnaise and salmon in a casserole dish. Top with cheese and bake for about 15 minutes or until bubbling and the top is golden brown. Let stand for 10 minutes before serving.

Enjoy!

Noodle Notes: ....

....

....

....

....

....

....

....

....

....

....

Super Luxe Seafood Mac & Cheese

From thought to pot to plate: 45 minutes

Serves: 4

Ingredients:

your favorite box of mac & cheese	1lb. of lobster meat, chopped
½ lb. of sea scallops, chopped	1 cup of shrimp, peeled and deveined
8 slices of bacon, chopped	½ cup of Gruyere cheese, grated
½ cup of Cheddar cheese, grated	½ teaspoon of nutmeg
2 teaspoons of dried tarragon	¼ teaspoon of cayenne pepper
dash of olive oil	salt and pepper to taste

Preheat oven to 350°F. Cook mac & cheese as directed on the box. Cook the bacon until crispy and set aside on a paper towel to drain. Combine salt, pepper, nutmeg, tarragon, cayenne pepper, Gruyere and Cheddar cheese by folding into the cooked mac & cheese. In a separate bowl, combine the lobster, shrimp, scallops and bacon. In a casserole dish combine the herbed mac & cheese mixture with the seafood/bacon mixture and bake for about 25 minutes or until bubbling and the top is golden brown. Let stand for 10 minutes before serving.

Put on your tiara for this dish!

Shrimp Scampi Mac & Cheese

From thought to pot to plate: 45 minutes
Serves: 2

Ingredients:

your favorite box of mac & cheese	1lb. large shrimp, peeled, deveined
3 tablespoons of butter	2 shallots, diced
2 cloves of garlic, minced	½ teaspoon of red pepper flakes
½ cup of white wine	1 can of diced tomatoes
juice and zest of one lemon	½ cup of basil leaves, chopped
salt and pepper to taste	

Cook mac & cheese as directed on the box. In a large skillet, sauté the shallots, garlic and red pepper flakes until soft. Add the shrimp and cook until opaque. Remove from pan and set aside. Add the wine, tomatoes and lemon juice to the skillet and bring the mixture to a boil. Reduce heat and let simmer for fifteen minutes. Return shrimp to the skillet and stir gently to combine. Serve on a bed of mac & cheese, garnish with basil.

Watch those guests scamper right to your table!

Noodle Notes: ....

....

....

....

....

....

....

....

....

....

....

Mac & Cheese Takes Veggies for a Spin

Alex's Vegan* Mac & Cheese

From thought to pot to plate: 35 minutes
Serves: 2

Ingredients:

2 cups of dried elbow macaroni	1 cup of soy Cheddar-flavored cheese
3 tablespoons of tapioca starch	1½ cups of vegetable stock
dash of olive oil	2 cups of soymilk
1 tablespoon of chili garlic sauce	1 tablespoon of hoisin sauce
1 tablespoon of paprika	1 small shallot, diced
1 cup of breadcrumbs	salt to taste

Preheat oven to 350°F. In a small bowl mix vegetable stock and the tapioca starch; set aside. Sauté the shallot in a little olive oil for 3 minutes and then add soymilk, hoisin sauce and garlic chili sauce. Add vegetable stock mixture and stir until the sauce thickens. Add half the grated cheese to the mixture and salt if needed. Cook and drain pasta when ready, return to pot and add cheese sauce, stir and transfer to a casserole dish. Sprinkle the rest of the cheese, paprika and breadcrumbs on top. Bake for about 15 minutes or until bubbling and the top is golden brown.

* You can do different variations of this dish adding vegetables, herbs, meatless chicken, seitan or tempeh – whatever is your favorite add-in.

Enjoy!

Balsamic Pumpkin Mac & Fontina Cheese

From thought to pot to plate: 40 minutes
Serves: 2

Ingredients:

your favorite box of mac & cheese	2 cups of pumpkin puree (unsweetened)
1 cup of yellow onion, diced	1 teaspoon of grainy mustard
salt and pepper to taste	1 teaspoon of dried thyme
1 cup of Fontina cheese, grated	1 teaspoon of balsamic vinegar
dash of olive oil	½ cup of breadcrumbs

Preheat oven to 350°F. Cook mac & cheese as directed on the box. In a heated skillet, sauté the onion in olive oil until soft and golden brown; then add the balsamic vinegar and reduce on low for about 10 minutes. In a casserole dish add the mustard, thyme, salt and pepper to the onions and combine with the mac & cheese and Fontina. Top with breadcrumbs and bake for about 15 minutes or until bubbling and the top is golden brown. Let stand for 10 minutes before serving.

Enjoy!

Noodle Notes: ....

....

....

....

....

....

....

....

....

....

....

Cheesy Crusty Crunch Mac & Cheese

From thought to pot to plate: 40 minutes

Serves: 2

Ingredients:

your favorite box of mac & cheese	dash of olive oil
1 cup of white onion, diced	4 cloves of garlic, minced
½ teaspoon of dry mustard	pinch of cayenne pepper
1 teaspoon of dried oregano	1 cup of Cheddar cheese, grated
1/3 cup of Greek style plain yogurt	salt and pepper to taste
1 cup of panko crumbs	½ cup of Parmesan cheese, grated
1/3 cup of water	

Preheat oven to 425°F. Cook mac & cheese as directed on the box. Sauté the onion, garlic, mustard, cayenne, oregano and then put in small saucepan with the water and bring to a boil. Whisk in the cheddar until melted; remove pan from heat and stir in the yogurt. Combine mixture with the mac & cheese, put in a greased casserole dish, top with Parmesan and panko and bake for about 15 minutes or until bubbling and the top is golden brown. Let stand for 10 minutes before serving.

Enjoy!

Crème Fraiche Mac & Cheese

From thought to pot to plate: 45 minutes

Serves: 2

Ingredients:

box of mac & white Cheddar cheese	1 cauliflower, cut into florets
tablespoon of olive oil	½ cup of Gruyere, grated
salt and pepper to taste	1 teaspoon of paprika
1 tablespoon of grainy mustard	1 cup of crème fraiche
1 cup of breadcrumbs	

Preheat oven to 400°F. Cook mac & cheese as directed on the box. Toss the cauliflower florets in olive oil and place on a sheet pan to roast. Remove and set aside. In a large bowl combine the mac & cheese, Gruyere, salt, pepper, paprika, mustard, crème fraiche and cauliflower. Transfer to a casserole dish and top with breadcrumbs. Bake for about 15 minutes or until bubbling and the top is golden brown. Let stand for 10 minutes before serving.

Enjoy!

Noodle Notes: ....

....

....

....

....

....

....

....

....

....

....

Crunchy Munchy Mac & Cheese

From thought to pot to plate: 45 minutes

Serves: 2

Ingredients:

your favorite box of mac & cheese	1½ cup of corn flakes, crumbled
1 cup of Cheddar cheese, grated	3 green onions, sliced
1 cup of Parmesan, grated	1 cup of panko breadcrumbs

Preheat oven to 350°F. Cook mac & cheese as directed on the box, then fold in corn flakes, green onions and Cheddar cheese and put in a casserole dish. Combine the Parmesan and panko breadcrumbs, sprinkle on top and bake in the oven for about 15 minutes or until bubbling and the top is golden brown. Let stand for 10 minutes before serving.

Enjoy!

Don't be a Square Mac & Cheese

From thought to pot to plate: 45 minutes

Serves: 6

Ingredients:

your favorite box of mac & cheese	2 cups of panko breadcrumbs
3 eggs, beaten	salt and pepper to taste
1 teaspoon of cayenne pepper	1 cup of flour
2 tablespoons of butter	

Cook mac & cheese as direct on the box. Spread mac & cheese in a baking dish and place in the refrigerator to cool for about 45 minutes. Once set, cut mac & cheese into squares. Dredge each square in a combination of salt, pepper, cayenne and flour, followed by egg coating and panko. In a hot skillet, melt butter and cook squares until brown on all sides.

Enjoy!

Dynamite Mac & Cheese

From thought to pot to plate: 25 minutes

Serves: 4

Ingredients:

your favorite box of mac & cheese	dash of olive oil
1/2 cup of carrot, shredded	2 cloves of garlic, minced
½ cup of white onion, diced	1/2 cup of zucchini, shredded
½ cup of frozen peas, thawed	½ cup of mozzarella cheese, grated
salt and pepper to taste	1/2 cup of frozen corn, thawed

Cook mac & cheese as directed on the box. In a large skillet, heat the oil and add the carrots, garlic, onion, zucchini, corn and peas. . Once cooked, add the vegetables to the mac & cheese, salt and pepper to taste and stir in the mozzarella.

Enjoy!

Noodle Notes: ....

....

....

....

....

....

....

....

....

....

....

....

....

Bring the Bling Mac & Cheese

From thought to pot to plate: 45 minutes
Serves: 2

Ingredients:

your favorite box of mac & cheese	4 leeks, washed, chopped
½ teaspoon of red pepper flakes	3 cloves of garlic, minced
salt and pepper to taste	dash of nutmeg
½ cup of fresh parsley, chopped	¼ cup of white wine
1 cup of breadcrumbs	½ cup of Parmesan cheese, grated
1 cup of Asiago cheese, grated	2 tablespoons of olive oil

Preheat oven to 375°F. Cook mac & cheese as directed on the box. Toss the chopped leeks in olive oil and sauté until golden brown. Add the pepper flakes, garlic, salt, pepper, nutmeg, parsley and white wine. Simmer on low until reduced – approximately 15 minutes; remove from heat. Place the breadcrumbs and Parmesan in a bowl, drizzled with olive oil and set aside. Combine mac & cheese, leek mixture and Asiago in a casserole dish and top with breadcrumb mixture. Bake for about 15 minutes or until bubbling and the top is golden brown. Let stand for 10 minutes before serving.

Enjoy!

Noodle Notes: ....
....
....
....
....
....
....
....
....
....

Garlicky Tomato Mac & Cheese

From thought to pot to plate: 35 minutes
Serves: 2

Ingredients:

your favorite box of mac & cheese	2 teaspoons of olive oil
½ cup of white onion, diced	2 cloves of garlic, minced
1 tablespoon of fresh parsley, chopped	1 teaspoon of dried oregano
salt and pepper to taste	3 tomatoes, chopped
½ teaspoon of crushed chilies	1 cup of breadcrumbs

Preheat oven to 375°F. Cook mac & cheese as directed on the box, In skillet, heat oil and sauté onion, garlic, parsley, oregano, salt and pepper. Add tomatoes and crushed chilies, cook until tomatoes reduce; about another five minutes. Take off heat. Toast breadcrumbs in the oven with a little olive oil for about 10 minutes, stirring often. Combine the mac & cheese with the seasoned vegetables and top with toasted breadcrumbs.

Enjoy!

Noodle Notes: ....

....

....

....

....

....

....

....

....

....

....

Casetta Mac & Cheese

From thought to pot to plate: 35 minutes
Serves: 2

Ingredients:

your favorite box of mac & cheese	½ teaspoon of dry mustard
salt and pepper to taste	2 green onions, sliced
½ teaspoon of paprika	½ cup of sour cream
1 cup of cottage cheese	dash of hot sauce
¼ cup of panko breadcrumbs	

Preheat oven to 350°F. Cook mac & cheese as directed on the box. Combine the mustard powder, salt, pepper, green onion and paprika, along with the sour cream and cottage cheese. Combine the dairy, spice mixture and hot sauce with the mac & cheese, put in a casserole dish and top with panko. Bake for about 15 minutes or until bubbling and the top is golden brown. Let stand for 10 minutes before serving.

Enjoy!

Noodle Notes: ....
....
....
....
....
....
....
....
....
....
....
....

Parsley Pesto Mac & Three Cheese Bake

From thought to pot to plate: 45 minutes

Serves: 2

Ingredients:

your favorite box of mac & cheese	salt and pepper to taste
dash of paprika	½ cup of Gruyere cheese, grated
½ cup of Swiss cheese, grated	1 bunch of fresh parsley, chopped
½ cup of walnuts, chopped	¼ cup of olive oil
1 cup of breadcrumbs	1 cup of Parmesan cheese, grated

Preheat oven to 375°F. Cook mac & cheese as directed on the box; then combine with salt, pepper, paprika, Gruyere and Swiss cheese. Put the parsley, walnuts and olive oil in the food processor and pulse together, then combine with mac & cheese mixture. Put in a casserole dish and top with breadcrumbs and Parmesan cheese. Bake for about 15 minutes or until bubbling and the top is golden brown. Let stand for 10 minutes before serving.

Enjoy!

Noodle Notes: ....

....

....

....

....

....

....

....

....

....

Harvest Time Mac & Cheese

From thought to pot to plate: 35 minutes

Serves: 2

Ingredients:

your favorite box of mac & cheese	2 tablespoons of butter
salt and pepper to taste	½ cup of walnuts, chopped
1 cup of pale ale	1 tablespoon of maple syrup
1 pinch of clove, ground	1 teaspoon of cayenne pepper
½ cup of fresh parsley, chopped	¼ teaspoon of paprika
½ teaspoon of fresh thyme, chopped	1 can of pumpkin puree (unsweetened)
½ cup of Parmesan cheese, grated	2 cups of Cheddar cheese, grated
1 cup of breadcrumbs	

Preheat oven to 350°F. Cook mac & cheese as directed on the box. In a heated saucepan, combine the butter, salt, pepper, walnuts, ale, maple syrup, clove, cayenne pepper, parsley, paprika and thyme. Stir until combined and then add pumpkin and Cheddar. Place in a casserole dish and top with Parmesan and breadcrumbs. Bake for about 15 minutes or until bubbling and the top is golden brown. Let stand for 10 minutes before serving.

Enjoy!

Italian Stallion Mac & Cheese

From thought to pot to plate: 45 minutes
Serves: 2

Ingredients:

your favorite box of mac & cheese	2 tablespoons of butter
2 cloves of garlic, minced	2 tablespoons of fresh basil, chopped
1 cup of heavy cream	1 cup of Parmesan cheese, grated
½ cup of goat cheese, crumbled	1 cup of panko breadcrumbs
½ cup of pesto (Recipes Reference)	salt and pepper to taste

Preheat oven to 350°F. Cook mac & cheese as directed on the box. Melt 2 tablespoons of butter in a pan and add garlic, basil and ¼ cup of Parmesan. Mix well and set aside. Put cream in a large saucepan and bring to a simmer over low heat until thickened slightly –about 6 minutes. Add the goat cheese and remaining Parmesan and whisk until melted; add mac & cheese and stir to coat, then the pesto, salt and pepper. Pour mixture into a casserole dish and top with panko. Bake for about 15 minutes or until bubbling and the top is golden brown. Let stand for 10 minutes before serving.

Enjoy!

Noodle Notes: ....

....

....

....

....

....

....

....

....

....

Cherry Pepper Mac & Cheese

From thought to pot to plate: 35 minutes

Serves: 2

Ingredients:

your favorite box of mac & cheese	1 chili pepper (pimiento), diced
4 cloves of garlic, minced	2 red peppers, diced
4 Manzanilla olives, pitted	2 tablespoons of mayonnaise
½ cup of Cheddar cheese, grated	salt and pepper to taste

Preheat oven to 350°F. Cook mac & cheese as directed on the box. Cook pimiento, garlic and peppers on medium heat in olive oil until soft. Combine the mac & cheese, red peppers mixture, olives and mayonnaise in a casserole dish along with the Cheddar. Bake for about 15 minutes or until bubbling and the top is golden brown. Let stand for 10 minutes before serving.

Enjoy!

Noodle Notes: ....
....
....
....
....
....
....
....
....
....
....
....
....
....

Woodland Mac & Cheese

From thought to pot to plate: 30 minutes
Serves: 2

Ingredients:

your favorite box of mac & cheese	6 spears of asparagus, trimmed
½ cup of ramps*, cleaned	salt and pepper to taste
2 tablespoons of butter	3 cloves of garlic, minced
1 tablespoon of grainy mustard	1 cup of Gruyere cheese, grated
½ cup of Swiss cheese, grated	

Cook mac & cheese as directed on the box. Melt butter in a skillet over medium heat and cook the asparagus and ramps with salt and pepper; add garlic and mustard. Combine the ramps and asparagus mixture with Gruyere and mac & cheese in a casserole dish; top with Swiss cheese. Bake for about 15 minutes or until bubbling and the top is golden brown. Let stand for 10 minutes before serving.

* Also known as wild leeks

Enjoy!

S'More Mac & Cheese

From thought to pot to plate: 15 minutes
Serves: 2

Ingredients:

your favorite box of mac & cheese	s'more mac & cheese

Cook mac & cheese as directed on the box, repeat.

Hope you are wearing your buffet pants!

Au Gratin Mac & Cheese

From thought to pot to plate: 50 minutes

Serves: 6

Ingredients:

your favorite box of mac & cheese	4 carrots, sliced on the diagonal
4 potatoes, peeled, thinly sliced	2 tablespoons of butter
1 white onion, sliced and separated	2 cloves of garlic, minced
¼ cup of flour	salt and pepper to taste
1 teaspoon of oregano	½ teaspoon of cayenne pepper
1½ cup of Cheddar cheese, grated	

Preheat oven to 375°F. Cook mac & cheese as directed on the box. Cook carrots and potatoes in a pot of boiling water until tender – about 8 minutes, then drain. Melt butter in a skillet and add the onion, garlic until soft, then add the flour and seasoning, mix well and combine with the mac & cheese. Put a layer of the mac & cheese mixture in a large casserole dish, followed by a layer of potatoes and carrots. Repeat both layers. Cover with cheese and bake for about 35 minutes or until bubbling and the top is golden brown. Let stand for 10 minutes before serving.

Enjoy!

Hearty Mac & Cheese

From thought to pot to plate: 35 minutes
Serves: 2

Ingredients:

your favorite box of mac & cheese	1 tablespoon of butter
2 cups of kale, chopped	3 cloves of garlic, minced
½ cup of red onion, diced	2 tablespoons of sun-dried tomato pesto
1 cup of plain yogurt	1 cup of chevre cheese
salt and pepper to taste	½ cup of Parmesan cheese, grated

Preheat oven to 350°F. Cook mac & cheese as directed on the box. In a large skillet, melt the butter and add the kale, garlic and onions. Cook until tender, and then add the pesto, yogurt, chevre, salt and pepper. Add the mac & cheese to the skillet and combine all of the ingredients. Sprinkle the top with Parmesan cheese and place skillet in the oven for 15 minutes until heated through. Serve.

Enjoy!

Noodle Notes: ....

....

....

....

....

....

....

....

....

....

....

....

Mac & Trio Cheese Minis

From thought to pot to plate: 40 minutes
Serves: 2

Ingredients:

your favorite box of mac & cheese	1 tablespoon of butter, melted
½ cup of Parmesan cheese, grated	½ teaspoon of paprika
salt and pepper to taste	¼ cup of Fontina cheese, grated
½ cup of Cheddar cheese, grated	¼ teaspoon of paprika
1 egg, beaten	

Preheat oven to 350°F. Cook mac & cheese as directed on the box. Brush 12 non-stick muffin tin portions with butter. Sprinkle with a tablespoon of Parmesan and tap out the excess. Combine the mac & cheese with the paprika, salt, pepper, egg, Fontina and Cheddar cheese. Spoon slightly rounded tablespoons of the macaroni into the prepared muffin cups, packing them gently. Sprinkle the remaining Parmesan on top of each cup. Bake the mini macs in the oven for about 15 minutes until golden and bubbling. Using a small spoon, carefully loosen the mini macs after letting them stand for 5 minutes before serving.

Enjoy!

Noodle Notes: ....
....
....
....
....
....
....
....
....
....

Herby Mushroom Mac & Cheese

From thought to pot to plate: 35 minutes
Serves: 2

Ingredients:

your favorite box of mac & cheese	dash of olive oil
½ cup of white onion, diced	2 cloves of garlic, minced
1 cup of dried mushrooms, chopped	1 cup of fresh mushrooms, sliced
½ cup of fresh parsley, chopped	¼ cup of fresh tarragon, chopped
1 cup of Swiss cheese, grated	½ cup of breadcrumbs
salt and pepper to taste	

Preheat oven to 350°F. Cook mac & cheese as directed on the box. In a heated skillet, cook the onion and garlic in olive oil until soft; add the mushrooms, parsley and tarragon for about another two minutes. Combine the mac & cheese, Swiss cheese and mushroom mixture in a casserole dish, top with breadcrumbs and bake for about 15 minutes or until bubbling and the top is golden brown. Let stand for 10 minutes before serving.

Enjoy!

Hippie Dippie Mac & Cheese

From thought to pot to plate: 25 minutes

Serves: 2

Ingredients:

your favorite box of mac & cheese	3 cloves of garlic, minced
3 ripe avocados, cut into chunks	3 teaspoons of fresh lime juice
½ cup of sour cream	1 cup of fresh cilantro, chopped
½ cup of red onion, diced	dash of olive oil
½ cup of pepper jack cheese, grated	

Cook mac & cheese as directed on the box. Place the garlic, red onion, olive oil, two avocadoes, lime juice, sour cream, cilantro, salt and pepper in a food processor and pulse until smooth. Put the jack cheese in a microwavable bowl and melt slightly – perhaps for 10 seconds. Combine the mac & cheese, pepper jack and the avocado sauce until coated and creamy and place in a serving dish. Garnish with fresh avocado chunks from the third avocado, and one last squeeze of lime. Serve warm.

Enjoy!

Noodle Notes: ....

....

....

....

....

....

....

....

....

....

....

....

Garden Variety Mac & Cheese

From thought to pot to plate: 45 minutes
Serves: 2

Ingredients:

box of mac & white Cheddar cheese	2 bell peppers, cut in strips
½ cup of white onion, diced	1 clove of garlic, minced
¼ cup of olive oil	1 tomato, peeled and chopped
4 leaves of fresh basil, chopped	salt and pepper to taste
2 tablespoons of hot water	

Cook mac & cheese as directed on the box. Heat oil in a frying pan and add onion, peppers and garlic, cook until soft. Add tomatoes, fresh basil and a little hot water to keep the mixture moist. Season to taste with salt and pepper then simmer for 10 minutes until the peppers are tender. Serve on a bed of mac & cheese.

Enjoy!

Noodle Notes:

Brocco-flower Mac & Cheese

From thought to pot to plate: 35 minutes
Serves: 2

Ingredients:

your favorite box of mac & cheese	dash of olive oil
1 clove of garlic, minced	½ cup of white onion, diced
1 cup of cauliflower, cut into florets	1 cup of broccoli, cut into florets
dash of nutmeg	salt and pepper to taste
½ cup of Swiss cheese, grated	

Preheat oven to 375°F. Cook mac & cheese as directed on the box. In a skillet, heat olive oil and sauté the garlic and white onion. In boiling water, cook the cauliflower and broccoli until just tender; drain and put in a casserole dish. Add the mac & cheese, vegetables, garlic, onions, nutmeg, salt and pepper. Sprinkle with grated Swiss cheese and bake for about 20 minutes or until bubbling and the top is golden brown. Let stand for 10 minutes before serving.

Enjoy!

Noodle Notes: ....
....
....
....
....
....
....
....
....
....
....
....

Cheezy Tomato Mac

From thought to pot to plate: 45 minutes
Serves: 2

Ingredients:

your favorite box of mac & cheese	½ cup of white onion, diced
1 cup of Fontina cheese, grated	½ cup of Parmesan cheese, grated
3 cloves of garlic, minced	dash of olive oil
1 firm tomato, sliced	½ cup of fresh basil, chopped
1 can of tomato soup	1 cup of breadcrumbs
salt and pepper to taste	

Preheat oven to 350°F. Cook mac & cheese as directed on the box. In skillet over medium heat, sauté onion and garlic in oil; add to the mac & cheese along with salt, pepper, basil and Fontina. Place in a casserole dish and pour tomato soup on top; let settle. Top with breadcrumbs, sliced tomatoes and Parmesan cheese. Bake for about 15 minutes or until bubbling and the top is golden brown. Let stand for 10 minutes before serving.

Enjoy!

Noodle Notes: ....
....
....
....
....
....
....
....
....
....

Double "S" Mac & Cheese

From thought to pot to plate: 35 minutes

Serves: 2

Ingredients:

your favorite box of mac & cheese	dash of olive oil
1 cup of fresh shallots, diced	2 cloves of garlic, minced
1 tablespoon of butter	¼ cup of fresh sage, chopped
2 cups of Gruyere cheese, grated	salt and pepper to taste

Preheat oven to 350°F. Cook mac & cheese as directed on the box. Heat olive oil over medium heat in a large pan, then add shallots and cook for about 4 minutes, stirring frequently, then add garlic to cook for another minute. Remove from the heat. Melt butter in the pan until nearly brown. Add sage and cook until crispy (about one minute) and season with salt and pepper. Mix mac & cheese, sage, onion and Gruyere in a casserole dish. Bake for about 15 minutes or until bubbling and the top is golden brown.

Enjoy!

Noodle Notes: ....

....

....

....

....

....

....

....

....

....

....

Deep Fried Mac & Cheese

From thought to pot to plate: 65 minutes
Serves: 6

Ingredients:

your favorite box of mac & cheese	1 cup of mozzarella, grated
1 cup of flour	2 eggs, beaten
2 cups of breadcrumbs	canola oil, for frying

Cook mac & cheese as directed on the box; fold in grated mozzarella. Pour into a 9"x 5" loaf pan, cover and refrigerate for about 45 minutes. When ready to fry the mac & cheese, put the flour, eggs and breadcrumbs in three shallow dishes. Heat the oil. Spoon the mac & cheese into individual portions; roll each into the flour, then the egg, followed by the breadcrumbs. Fry in hot oil until crispy, turning once or twice. Transfer to paper towels to drain. Serve warm.

Delicious savory or sweet! Enjoy!

Noodle Notes: ....

....

....

....

....

....

....

....

....

....

....

....

....

Mac and Leek

From thought to pot to plate: 25 minutes

Serves: 2

Ingredients:

your favorite box of mac & cheese	1 leek, washed, chopped
salt and pepper to taste	1 tablespoon of butter

Cook mac & cheese as directed on the box. In a large skillet, melt the butter on medium heat and add the leek – cook until tender and add to the finished mac & cheese.

Its mac and leek time! Don't worry you really don't need to go to the washroom…

Ring the Bell Mac & Cheese

From thought to pot to plate: 35 minutes

Serves: 2

Ingredients:

box of mac & white Cheddar cheese	dash of olive oil
3 orange peppers, chopped	1 clove of garlic, minced
½ cup of white onion, diced	1 large tomato, chopped
handful of fresh basil, chopped	½ cup of vegetable broth
salt and pepper to taste	

Cook mac & cheese as directed on the box. Heat the oil in a frying pan and add the chopped peppers, minced garlic and white onion until lightly browned. Add the chopped tomatoes, basil and broth. Season with salt and pepper and simmer for 10 minutes until peppers are tender. Combine mixture with the mac & cheese.

Enjoy!

Noodle Notes: ....

....

....

....

....

....

....

....

....

....

....

....

Zany Zucchini Mac & Cheese

From thought to pot to plate: 35 minutes
Serves: 2

Ingredients:

your favorite box of mac & cheese	2 zucchinis, grated with peel on
dash of olive oil	2 cloves of garlic, minced
½ cup of white onion, diced	1 egg, beaten
salt and pepper to taste	½ cup of Cheddar cheese, grated

Preheat oven to 350°F. Drain the grated zucchini in a colander for half an hour, pressing gently to remove excess water. Cook mac & cheese as directed on the box. In a large skillet, heat olive oil and sauté the garlic and onion, then add the drained zucchini and simmer for about 2 minutes – until soft. Drain excess liquid again in a colander. Combine the zucchini mixture with a beaten egg, salt, pepper and the mac & cheese and place in casserole dish. Top the dish with Cheddar and bake for about 20 minutes or until bubbling and the top is golden brown. Let stand for 10 minutes before serving.

Enjoy!

Noodle Notes: ....

....

....

....

....

....

....

....

....

....

....

Luv Boat Mac & Cheese

From thought to pot to plate: 45 minutes
Serves: 4

Ingredients:

your favorite box of mac & cheese	4 medium sized zucchini
½ cup of white onion, diced	½ cup of tomato sauce
salt and pepper to taste	1 cup of Monterey Jack cheese, grated
½ cup of breadcrumbs	

Preheat oven to 350°F. Cook mac & cheese as directed on the box. Cut zucchini in half lengthwise; cut a thin slice from the bottom of each to allow zucchini to sit flat. Scoop out most of the zucchini flesh. Place shells in the microwave on high for 2 minutes, drain and set aside. In a large skillet, cook zucchini flesh (chopped) and onion together until soft. Stir in the tomato sauce, salt and pepper and about 2 cups of mac & cheese. Spoon mixture into zucchini shells and top with Monterey Jack and breadcrumbs. Bake for about 15 minutes or until bubbling and the tops are golden brown.

Enjoy!

Noodle Notes: ....

....

....

....

....

....

....

....

....

....

....

....

Power-up Mac & Cheese

From thought to pot to plate: 40 minutes

Serves: 2

Ingredients:

your favorite box of mac & cheese	1 medium butternut squash
3 cups of spinach, chopped	3 cloves of garlic, minced
¾ cup of white onion, diced	2 cups of Gouda cheese, grated
½ cup of plain yogurt	salt and pepper to taste
dash of olive oil	

Preheat oven to 350°F. Cook mac & cheese as directed on the box. Cut squash in half, scoop out seeds and roast upside down on sheet pan for about 15 minutes to soften (put about 1 cm of water on sheet to keep from burning). In a large skillet, heat olive oil and add the garlic, onion, salt and pepper; cook until soft. Remove the squash from the oven, peel and cut into bite-sized pieces. Add to the onions and sauté for 10 minutes, adding stemmed and chopped spinach for the last minute to wilt. Combine mixture with the mac & cheese. Add 1½ cup of Gouda cheese and the yogurt. Transfer mixture to casserole dish, sprinkling the rest of the Gouda on the top. Bake for about 15 minutes or until bubbling and the top is golden brown. Let stand for 10 minutes before serving.

Enjoy!

Magic Mushroom Mac & Cheese

From thought to pot to plate: 35 minutes

Serves: 2

Ingredients:

your favorite box of mac & cheese	1 tablespoon of butter
3 cloves of garlic, minced	3 green onions, sliced
½ cup of white onion, diced	4 cups of mushrooms, sliced
1 cup of parsley, chopped	1 egg, beaten
salt and pepper to taste	½ cup of Swiss cheese
1 cup of breadcrumbs	

Preheat oven to 350°F. Cook mac & cheese as directed on the box. In a skillet melt butter and sauté the garlic, onions, mushrooms and parsley. Combine the mushroom mixture with a beaten egg, salt, pepper and the mac & cheese; place in casserole dish. Top the dish with breadcrumbs and Swiss cheese and bake for about 20 minutes or until bubbling and the top is golden brown. Let stand for 10 minutes before serving.

Enjoy!

Noodle Notes: ....

....

....

....

....

....

....

....

....

....

....

Mint Cilantro Mac & Cheese

From thought to pot to plate: 25 minutes
Serves: 2

Ingredients:

your favorite box of mac & cheese	dash of olive oil
1 jalapeno, diced	salt to taste
1 cup of fresh mint, chopped	1 cup of fresh cilantro, chopped
1 teaspoon of fresh ginger, grated	¼ cup of lemon juice

Cook mac & cheese as directed on the box. In a food processor, combine the olive oil, jalapeno, salt, mint, cilantro, ginger and lemon juice and pulse until blended. Fold into the mac & cheese. Serve hot.

Enjoy!

Health Nut Mac & Cheese

From thought to pot to plate: 35 minutes
Serves: 2

Ingredients:

your favorite box of mac & cheese	2 potatoes, thinly sliced
1 cup of green beans, in 2" pieces	1 cup of Parmesan cheese, grated
1½ cups of pesto (Recipes Reference)	salt and pepper to taste

Cook pasta until tender, drain and save the cooking water (*reserve the cheese powder for another use*) to boil potatoes and beans until tender. Put macaroni, potatoes and green beans in a large bowl; add pesto and cheese and toss together gently, seasoning to taste. Serve warm or chilled.

Buon appetito!

Puttin' on the Ritz Mac & Cheese Pie

From thought to pot to plate: 35 minutes

Serves: 2

Ingredients:

your favorite box of mac & cheese	1½ cup of Cheddar cheese, grated
2 eggs, beaten	½ cup of milk
¼ cup of sour cream	2 tablespoons of cold butter, cut in pieces
salt and pepper to taste	1½ cups of crackers, crushed
1 teaspoon of red pepper flakes	2 tablespoons of sugar
½ cup of butter, melted	

Preheat oven to 350°F. Cook mac & cheese as directed on the box, add ½ cup of the Cheddar cheese to the prepared macaroni. In another bowl, whisk together eggs, milk, sour cream, cold butter pieces, salt and pepper. Stir milk and egg mixture into the mac & cheese. For the piecrust, mix together cracker crumbs, red pepper flakes and sugar. Pour in melted butter and mix together with a fork until moistened. Press into the bottom and sides of a 9" pie plate. Stir the milk mixture into the mac & cheese and add to piecrust. Sprinkle remaining Cheddar over pie and bake for about 20 to 25 minutes or until the cheese is browned and slightly crispy. Serve warm.

Enjoy!

Mac & Cheese Arrosto

From thought to pot to plate: 50 minutes
Serves: 2

Ingredients:

your favorite box of mac & cheese	½ cup of zucchini, in bite-sized pieces
½ cup of red onion, in bite-sized pieces	3 cloves of garlic, peeled
2 carrots, peeled, in bite-sized pieces	other vegetables good roasted
olive oil to coat vegetables	½ teaspoon of cayenne pepper
1 teaspoon of balsamic vinegar	salt and pepper to taste

Preheat oven to 350°F. Toss prepared vegetables in a baking dish with seasoning, balsamic vinegar and olive oil until coated. Roast in the oven for 35 minutes until tender. Cook mac & cheese as directed on the box; serve roasted vegetables on a bed of mac & cheese.

Enjoy!

Noodle Notes: ....
....
....
....
....
....
....
....
....
....
....
....
....

Triple Threat Mac & Cheese

From thought to pot to plate: 35 minutes

Serves: 2

Ingredients:

your favorite box of mac & cheese	1 small red onion, sliced
4 cloves of garlic, minced	¼ cup of white wine
1 teaspoon of dry mustard	1 tablespoon of fresh sage, chopped
salt and pepper to taste	2 tablespoons of cream cheese
1 cup of Stilton cheese, crumbled	2 cups of butternut squash, chopped
1 cup of breadcrumbs	dash of olive oil

Preheat oven to 350°F. In a heated skillet, sauté the sliced onion and garlic in olive oil until tender. Add wine, mustard and sage; season with salt and pepper and simmer for another minute. Mix together mac & cheese, onion mixture, cream cheese and Stilton; fold in cooked squash and transfer to a casserole dish. Top with breadcrumbs and bake for about 15 minutes or until bubbling and the top is golden brown. Let stand for 10 minutes before serving.

Enjoy!

Noodle Notes: ....

....

....

....

....

....

....

....

....

....

Classic Combo Mac & Cheese

From thought to pot to plate: 35 minutes

Serves: 2

Ingredients:

your favorite box of mac & cheese	dash of olive oil
1 cup of white onion, diced	3 cloves of garlic, minced
1 jar of marinated artichokes, drained	bunch of fresh spinach
½ cup of Fontina cheese, grated	½ teaspoon of nutmeg
salt and pepper to taste	½ cup of Parmesan cheese, grated

Preheat oven to 350°F. Cook mac & cheese as directed on the box. In a large skillet heat olive oil on medium heat and sauté the onion and garlic until soft, then add artichokes and rinsed and stemmed spinach until spinach is wilted. Mix in the Fontina and nutmeg until incorporated. Season with salt and pepper and place mixture in casserole dish, topped with Parmesan cheese. Bake for about 20 minutes or until bubbling and the top is golden brown. Let stand for 5 minutes before serving.

Enjoy!

Noodle Notes: ....

....

....

....

....

....

....

....

....

....

....

Sunny Outlook Mac & Cheese

From thought to pot to plate: 35 minutes
Serves: 2

Ingredients:

your favorite box of mac & cheese	1 yellow pepper, sliced
1 small yellow zucchini, sliced	salt and pepper to taste
1 yellow tomato, sliced	1 cup of mozzarella, grated
dash of olive oil	

Preheat oven to 350°F. Cook mac & cheese as directed on the box. In a skillet sauté pepper and zucchini until soft. Combine vegetables with mac & cheese, salt and pepper in a casserole dish and layer the top with slices of yellow tomato and mozzarella cheese. Bake for about 15 minutes or until bubbling and the top is golden brown. Let stand for 10 minutes before serving.

Enjoy!

Noodle Notes: ....

....

....

....

....

....

....

....

....

....

....

....

....

Vitamin C Booster Mac & Cheese

From thought to pot to plate: 40 minutes
Serves: 2

Ingredients:

your favorite box of mac & cheese	¾lb. of carrots, peeled, thinly sliced
juice of one lemon	¼ cup of water
1 orange pepper, diced	1 tablespoon of fresh tarragon, chopped
salt and pepper to taste	½ cup of Cheddar cheese, grated
½ cup of breadcrumbs	

Preheat oven to 350°F. Cook mac & cheese as directed on the box. In a saucepan combine the carrots, lemon juice and ¼ cup of water. Bring to a boil; then cover and simmer over moderate heat until the carrots are soft. Transfer to a blender and puree until smooth. Combine the puree with mac & cheese with the diced orange pepper, tarragon, salt and pepper and put in a casserole dish. Top with Cheddar and bread-crumbs and bake for about 15 minutes or until bubbling and the top is golden brown. Let stand for 5 minutes before serving.

Basically a spa treatment.

Noodle Notes: ....
....
....
....
....
....
....
....
....
....
....

OMG Pear Rosemary Mac & Gorgonzola

From thought to pot to plate: 35 minutes
Serves: 2

Ingredients:

your favorite box of mac & cheese	1 teaspoon of butter
1 teaspoon of rosemary, chopped	½ cup of white onion, diced
2 cloves of garlic, minced	2 pears, sliced
salt and pepper to taste	1 cup of Gorgonzola, crumbled

Preheat oven to 350°F. Cook mac & cheese as directed on the box. In a skillet on medium heat melt the butter and add the rosemary, onion and garlic, cook until soft. Add the pears and sauté for about three more minutes. Add salt, pepper and half of the Gorgonzola a bit at a time until melted. Combine the mixture with the mac & cheese in a greased casserole dish, top with the other ½ of the Gorgonzola and bake for 15 minutes or until bubbling and golden brown. Let stand for ten minutes before serving.

Enjoy!

Noodle Notes:

Mac & Cheese Gets Dressed Up

Thanksgiving Mac & Cheese

From thought to pot to plate: 45 minutes

Serves: 2

Ingredients:

box of mac & white Cheddar cheese	½ cup of pancetta, chopped
2 cups of Brussels sprouts	½ cup of dried cranberries
1 small Vidalia onion, diced	½ teaspoon of red pepper flakes
salt and pepper to taste	½ cup of Cheddar cheese, grated
1 teaspoon of grainy mustard	1 cup of breadcrumbs
1 teaspoon of butter	dash of olive oil
½ cup of fresh parsley, chopped	1 teaspoon of balsamic vinegar

Preheat oven to 350°F. Cook mac & cheese as directed on the box. Peel off outer leaves of Brussels sprouts and boil until tender (not overcooked!). Remove from heat, rinse in cold water and quarter. In a large skillet cook the pancetta until crispy; remove from heat and set on paper towel to drain. Sauté the onion in olive oil, salt, pepper and red pepper flakes until soft. Add the balsamic vinegar and Brussels sprouts to caramelize, and then add the cranberries. Remove mixture from heat. Combine the butter, parsley and breadcrumbs and sauté in pan until golden brown. Combine the onion and Brussels sprouts mixture, pancetta, mustard and mac & cheese in a casserole dish. Top with breadcrumbs and Cheddar and bake for about 15 minutes or until bubbling and the top is golden brown. Let stand for 5 minutes before serving.

Eat your sprouts!

Happy New Year Mac & Cheese

From thought to pot to plate: 20 minutes
Serves: 2

Ingredients:

your favorite box of mac & cheese	2 goose breasts
¾ cup of white wine	3 shallots, diced
3 cloves of garlic, minced	1 stalk of celery, chopped
1 tablespoon of poultry seasoning	salt and pepper to taste
dash of olive oil	

Cook mac & cheese as directed on the box. Sauté the goose (cut into thin strips across the grain) in the olive oil in a large skillet, and add the garlic, shallots, celery, poultry season and wine and simmer for 10 minutes. Combine mixture with mac & cheese and salt and pepper to taste.

Bottoms up to Mac & Cheese 365!

Valentine's Day Mac & Cheese

From thought to pot to plate: 25 minutes
Serves: 2

Ingredients:

your favorite box of mac & cheese	½ lb. of cherries, pitted, stemmed
1 cup of cream cheese	salt and pepper to taste

Cook mac & cheese as directed on the box. Add the cherries and cream cheese. Stir to combine. Impress your honey.

"All you need is love. But a little chocolate now and then doesn't hurt." – C. M. Schultz

St. Patrick's Day Mac & Cheese

From thought to pot to plate: 25 minutes

Serves: 2

Ingredients:

your favorite box of mac & cheese	1 teaspoon of green food coloring
2 cans of Guinness	

Cook mac & cheese as directed on the box. Stir in the green food coloring. Serve with Guinness.

"May your home always be too small to hold your friends." - Irish toast

Easter Mac & Cheese

From thought to pot to plate: 55 minutes

Serves: 2

Ingredients:

your favorite box of mac & cheese	1 cup of cooked ham, cubed
2 cups of celery, chopped	3 green onions, sliced
1 cup of broccoli, cut into florets	¼ cup of red onion, diced
½ cup of mayonnaise	dash of celery salt
salt and pepper to taste	

Cook mac & cheese as directed on the box. Refrigerate until cold – about 50 minutes. Add the vegetables, ham, mayonnaise and other ingredients and combine. Chill until ready to serve.

Feel virtuous. Eat salad.

O Canada Mac & Cheese Salad

From thought to pot to plate: 50 minutes
Serves: 2

Ingredients:

box of mac & white Cheddar cheese	2 cups of cherry tomatoes
2 red peppers, chopped	½ cup of red onion, diced
dash of olive oil	2 cloves of garlic, minced
1 teaspoon of white balsamic vinegar	1 cup of chevre, crumbled
salt and pepper to taste	

Preheat oven to 350°F. Place the tomatoes, garlic, red onion and red peppers in roasting dish; add a dash of olive oil to lightly coat, then roast in the oven for about 35 minutes. Cook mac & cheese as directed on the box. Set aside to chill. Once vegetables are roasted, set aside to cool, and then fold the cooled vegetables into the mac & cheese with a dash of olive oil, 1 teaspoon of white balsamic vinegar, crumbled chevre and salt and pepper to taste. Serve cold.

Break out the mac and canoes - it's Canada Day!

Noodle Notes: ....

....

....

....

....

....

....

....

....

....

....

Red, White and Bleu Mac & Cheese Salad

From thought to pot to plate: 45 minutes

Serves: 2

Ingredients:

box of mac & white Cheddar cheese	1 clove of garlic, minced
½ cup of red onion, diced	2 tablespoons of mayonnaise
salt and pepper to taste	1 cup of blue cheese, crumbled

Cook mac & cheese as directed on the box. Place in refrigerator to cool. In a large bowl, combine the diced red onion, minced garlic, bleu cheese, mayonnaise, salt and pepper. Once cool, combine the mac & cheese in the same bowl and serve as a cold side dish.

There's always something to celebrate with mac & cheese!

Noodle Notes: ....

....

....

....

....

....

....

....

....

....

....

....

....

....

....

Jack O' Lantern Mac & Cheese

From thought to pot to plate: 40 minutes
Serves: 2

Ingredients:

your favorite box of mac & cheese	2 small pumpkins, cleaned
salt and pepper to taste	½ teaspoon of garlic powder
¼ teaspoon of cayenne pepper	dash of olive oil

Preheat oven to 400°F. Place pumpkins on sheet pan and roast until tender (25 minutes) Remove from oven and cool for 15 minutes. Slice the top off and set aside. Scoop out seeds and pulp leaving a 1" interior border. Clean the pumpkin seeds and toss in a little olive oil, salt, pepper and cayenne. Place on a sheet pan to roast. Cook mac & cheese as directed on the box; adding chopped pumpkin flesh is an option. Once cooked, spoon into the pumpkins and sprinkle roasted pumpkin seeds on top.

* You may find there aren't many seeds in the small pumpkins, if so save seeds from larger ones to make this recipe.

Very scary!

Noodle Notes: ....

....

....

....

....

....

....

....

....

....

....

Season's Greetings Mac & Cheese

From thought to pot to plate: 45 minutes
Serves: 2

Ingredients:

your favorite box of mac & cheese	2 turkey breasts, in bite-sized pieces
¼ cup of dried cranberries	1 cup of prepared stuffing
½ cup of white onion, diced	2 cloves of garlic, minced
dash of olive oil	salt and pepper to taste

Cook mac & cheese as directed on the box. Sauté the turkey, onions and garlic in a dash of olive oil for approximately 10 minutes or until cooked. Add cranberries, the stuffing and salt and pepper to taste. Serve on a bed of mac & cheese.

This dish will be your Uncle Normie's favorite! Pass the egg nog!

Noodle Notes: ....

....

....

....

....

....

....

....

....

....

....

....

....

....

Smacwiches

Mac & Cheese Clubhouse

From thought to pot to plate: 50 minutes
Serves: 2

Ingredients:

your favorite box of mac & cheese	1 chicken breast
4 slices of smoked bacon	2 slices of Monterey Jack cheese
2 slices of tomato	salt and pepper to taste
2 slices of red onion	1 avocado, sliced
6 slices of bread, toasted	mayonnaise
grainy mustard	4 leaves of bib lettuce

Cook mac & cheese as directed on the box. Once cooked, set in a loaf pan and refrigerate for about 45 minutes. Cook bacon in a large nonstick skillet over medium heat until crisp; remove from pan and set aside on paper towel to drain. Add chicken to the pan and cook. Build your sandwich; put mayonnaise on one slice of bread, and mustard on another. Stack avocado, chicken, bacon, onion, tomato and cheese on one "deck" then slice a piece of mac & cheese off your chilled batch and heat in a buttered skillet. Complete your sandwich with the heated slice of mac & cheese as the other "deck". Slice in half and skewer with long toothpicks to serve.

You'll always be part of the club with this sandwich!

Philly Mac & Cheese Steak Wonder

From thought to pot to plate: 35 minutes
Serves: 4

Ingredients:

your favorite box of mac & cheese	2 beef sirloins, cut into strips
½ cup of fresh mushrooms, sliced	1 green pepper, s sliced
1 small white onion, sliced	¼ cup of your favorite BBQ sauce
1 teaspoon of mayonnaise	4 cheese slices
4 good-sized hoagie buns	

Preheat oven to 350°F. Cook mac & cheese as directed on the box. In a skillet cook the steak to your liking, stir in BBQ sauce to coat (reserve about a teaspoon of BBQ sauce to add to mayonnaise). Remove steak from skillet and set aside. In the same pan, sauté the peppers, onion and mushrooms until tender. Place your hoagie buns open faced on a sheet pan. Combine the reserved BBQ sauce and mayonnaise and spread on the buns, followed by a spoonful of mac & cheese, and the beef strip, sautéed peppers, onions and mushrooms mixture. Top each bun with a slice of cheese and bake for about 15 minutes or until bubbling and the top is golden brown.

Practically the eighth wonder of the world!

Bacon, Avocado and PB Mac & Cheese

From thought to pot to plate: 30 minutes
Serves: 2

Ingredients:

your favorite box of mac & cheese	2 tbsp. of crunchy peanut butter
3 slices of bacon, chopped	1 avocado, sliced

Cook mac & cheese as directed on the box. Cook the bacon in a skillet until crispy and set aside on a paper towel to drain. Combine mac & cheese, bacon and peanut butter in a serving dish and top with sliced avocado.

You will not believe how good this is!

Mac & Cheese Meatball Subs

From thought to pot to plate: 30 minutes
Serves: 4

Ingredients:

your favorite box of mac & cheese	½lb. of lean ground beef
1 cup of tomato sauce	dash of hot sauce
¼ of BBQ sauce	salt and pepper to taste
1 tablespoon of olive oil	4 sub buns, partially split
1 cup of mozzarella cheese, grated	

Preheat oven to 350°F. Cook mac & cheese as directed on the box. In a large bowl, combine the beef with the mac & cheese, hot sauce, BBQ sauce, salt and pepper. Form balls and cook in an oiled skillet on medium-high high. Place the sub buns open-faced on a sheet pan. Put cooked mac & cheese meatballs on top, followed by a spoonful of tomato sauce and a sprinkle of mozzarella. Baked until heated through, the cheese is bubbling and the top is golden brown.

There's no substituting this sandwich!

Grilled Mac & Cheese Smacwich

From thought to pot to plate: 25 minutes
Serves: 2

Ingredients:

your favorite box of mac & cheese	4 slices of your favorite bread
1 tablespoon of butter	2 slices of Cheddar cheese

Cook mac & cheese as directed on the box. Butter outside of bread slices; spread desired amount of mac and cheese on inside, top with a slice of cheddar and cover with other slice of bread. Grill the sandwich until both sides are golden brown and the cheese is melted, turning once.

Mac & Cheese Joes

From thought to pot to plate: 30 minutes

Serves: 4

Ingredients:

your favorite box of mac & cheese	2lb. of lean ground beef
1 cup of your favorite BBQ sauce	½ cup of white onion, diced
4 large hamburger buns	4 slices of Cheddar cheese

Preheat oven to 350°F. Cook mac & cheese as directed on the box. Heat a oil in a large pan and brown onions; add beef and sauté until cooked through. Pour in BBQ sauce and combine. Place hamburger buns open faced on a sheet pan; spoon the mac & cheese on the buns and then layer on the beef mixture and top with a slice of Cheddar cheese. Bake for about 15 minutes or until bubbling and the top is golden brown.

Now we're talking!

Mac & Cheese with Turkey and Cheddar

From thought to pot to plate: 25 minutes

Serves: 2

Ingredients:

your favorite box of mac & cheese	4 slices of bread, toasted
two teaspoons of mayonnaise	½ lb. smoked turkey breast, sliced
4 slices of Cheddar cheese	½ head of lettuce, shredded
salt and pepper to taste	1 granny smith apple, thinly sliced

Cook mac & cheese as directed on the box. Make your sandwiches loaded with mayonnaise, turkey breast, Cheddar, lettuce and apple slices. Salt and pepper to taste; serve on the side with mac & cheese.

Enjoy!

Monto Cristo Mac & Cheese

From thought to pot to plate: 45 minutes

Serves: 4

Ingredients:

your favorite box of mac & cheese	4 slices of black forest ham
4 slices of cooked turkey meat	4 slices of Swiss cheese
8 slices of your favorite bread	1 teaspoon of mayonnaise
1 teaspoon of grainy mustard	1 egg, beaten
½ of cup milk	2 teaspoons of butter
salt and pepper to taste	

Cook mac & cheese as directed on the box. Spread bread with mayonnaise and mustard. Alternate ham, Swiss and turkey slices on bread. Combine the egg, milk, salt and pepper in a bowl and dredge each sandwich in the mixture. Heat a buttered skillet over medium heat; brown the sandwich on both sides – turning once. Serve hot with a side of mac & cheese.

Served with a Monte Cristo coffee? Don't mind if I do!

Enjoy!

Noodle Notes:

Elvis Has Left the Building Mac & Cheese

From thought to pot to plate: 30 minutes
Serves: 2

Ingredients:

your favorite box of mac & cheese	½ cup of crunchy peanut butter
1 ripe banana, sliced	4 pieces of thickly sliced white bread
2 teaspoons of honey	4 slices of bacon
1 tablespoon of butter	

Cook mac & cheese as directed on the box. In a skillet, cook bacon slices until crispy and set aside on a paper towel to drain. Place two slices of bread on a board and build the sandwich with a thin layer of peanut butter, a drizzle of honey, banana and a scoop of mac & cheese. Top with second slice of bread, coat outsides of sandwiches with butter and grill in a pan until both sides are golden brown, flipping the sandwich once – approximately 3 or 4 minutes a side.

Can't help falling in love… with this sandwich!

Noodle Notes: ....

....

....

....

....

....

....

....

....

....

....

....

Meatloaf Mac & Grilled Cheese Smacwich

From thought to pot to plate: 75 minutes
Serves: 6

Ingredients:

your favorite box of mac & cheese	2lbs. of lean ground beef
1 egg, lightly beaten	1 cup of white onion, diced
1 teaspoon of oregano	¼ cup of ketchup
2 tablespoons of Worcestershire sauce	2 tablespoons of prepared mustard
1 cup of dried breadcrumbs	12 slices of bread
2 tablespoons of butter	

Preheat oven to 350°F. Cook mac & cheese as directed on the box and then press into a greased 9"x 5" loaf pan, then put in the refrigerator for one hour to set. Combine the ground beef, onion, oregano, ketchup, Worcestershire sauce, mustard, breadcrumbs and egg and press into a second greased 9"x 5" loaf pan. Bake meatloaf for approximately 55 minutes. Once the meatloaf is cooked, let stand to set before removing. Butter one side of each piece of bread. Slice ½' thick pieces of meatloaf and a ½" thick slice of mac & cheese to make your sandwich, then grill in your hot pan with the buttered sides on the heat, until bread is brown and mac & cheese is heated through.

Great with mustard! Enjoy!

California Dreamin' Mac & Cheese

From thought to pot to plate: 35 minutes
Serves: 4

Ingredients:

your favorite box of mac & cheese	2 chicken breasts
3 avocados, sliced	4 slices of Monterey Jack cheese
1 small red onion, sliced	4 ciabatta buns
2 teaspoons of mayonnaise	several spinach leaves
dash of olive oil	salt and pepper to taste

Cook mac & cheese as directed on the box. Cook the chicken in a skillet with olive oil. Once thoroughly cooked, transfer to cutting board and slice. Prepare the sandwich by slicing the ciabatta and filling evenly with mac & cheese, chicken, spinach, red onion, avocado, cheese, salt and pepper. Grill until melted and cooked evenly on both sides.

Enjoy!

Posh Mac & Cheese Smacwich

From thought to pot to plate: 30 minutes
Serves: 2

Ingredients:

your favorite box of mac & cheese	1 ripe pear, cored and sliced
4 slices of French bread, bias cut	4 slices of bacon
2 slices of Brie cheese, sliced	2 tablespoons of butter

Cook mac & cheese as directed on the box. Cook the slices of bacon in a skillet until crispy and drain on a paper towel. Assemble the sandwiches; layer the bacon, pear, Brie and a spoonful of mac & cheese. Butter the outsides of the bread and cook in a skillet until golden brown on both sides, flipping once.

Enjoy!

ABC's Grilled Mac & Cheese Smacwich

From thought to pot to plate: 20 minutes
Serves: 4

Ingredients:

your favorite box of mac & cheese	2 avocados, sliced
8 slices of bacon	4 slices of Cheddar cheese
1 tablespoon of mayonnaise	8 slices of your favorite bread
salt and pepper to taste	

Cook mac & cheese as directed on the box. Cook bacon until crispy and set aside on paper towel to drain. Toast the bread, spread four slices with mayonnaise and build your sandwich using sliced avocado, crispy bacon, a spoonful of mac & cheese and sliced Cheddar cheese. Salt and pepper to taste.

Coming soon, the mac & cheese alphabet!

BBQ Mac & Cheese Burgers

From thought to pot to plate: 35 minutes
Serves: 4

Ingredients:

your favorite box of mac & cheese	1lb. of lean ground beef
½ cup of white onion, diced	4 of your favorite burger buns
2 tablespoons of BBQ sauce	pepper to taste

Cook mac & cheese as directed on the box. Mix together the ground beef and onion; shape into patties and put on preheated grill. Once one side is cooked (when juices pool on the top side), flip and add a scoop of mac & cheese, topped with BBQ sauce. Serve on toasted buns with your favorite condiments.

Why have just a burger when you can have a BBQ mac & cheese burger?

Croque Monsieur Mac & Cheese

From thought to pot to plate: 35 minutes

Serves: 2

Ingredients:

your favorite box of mac & cheese	2 tablespoons of butter
2 tablespoons of flour	1 cup of milk
pinch of nutmeg	8 slices of firm white bread
2 teaspoons of Dijon mustard	4 slices of Black Forest ham
4 slices of Swiss cheese	½ cup of Gruyere cheese, grated
2 teaspoons of tarragon, chopped	salt and pepper to taste

Cook mac & cheese as directed on the box. Melt 1½ tablespoons of butter in small saucepan over medium heat. Add flour and stir for one minute and gradually whisk in milk. Add nutmeg, salt and pepper. Increase heat to medium-high and boil until sauce thickens, whisking constantly for about two minutes. Set sauce aside in a small bowl. Preheat broiler. Place two slices of bread on a cutting board and top each with mustard, one slice of Swiss and one slice of ham, then top with other slices of bread. Brush with the remaining butter and add to skillet, cooking until golden brown. Transfer to a sheet pan, pour over sauce, sprinkle with cheese and broil for about 2 minutes. Serve garnished with chopped tarragon and a side of mac & cheese.

Bon appétit!

Rock Star Mac & Cheese Smacwich

From thought to pot to plate: 55 minutes
Serves: 4

Ingredients:

your favorite box of mac & cheese	2 tablespoons of butter
1 small white onion, sliced	2 cups of pulled pork
1 cup of BBQ sauce	4 slices of Cheddar cheese
8 slices of sourdough bread	2 green onions, sliced
salt and pepper to taste	

Preheat oven to 350°F. Cook mac & cheese as directed on the box. Place in loaf pan, cover and put in the refrigerator for about 45 minutes. Slice chilled mac like a loaf of bread. In a skillet, melt a teaspoon of butter and cook the onions until soft and caramelized; add salt, pepper, green onion, pulled pork and BBQ sauce. Butter the outsides of all of the bread and build the sandwich with a slice of the chilled mac & cheese, a slice of Cheddar and the BBQ pulled pork and onions. Grill in a skillet until both sides are golden brown, turning once.

Enjoy!

Noodle Notes: ....

....

....

....

....

....

....

....

....

....

Croque Señor Mac & Cheese Havana

From thought to pot to plate: 45 minutes

Serves: 4

Ingredients:

your favorite box of mac & cheese	8 slices of black forest ham
4 slices of Swiss cheese	1 tablespoon of red wine vinegar
½ cup of green olives, pitted	½ cup of raisins
2 green onions, sliced	dash of olive oil
1 tablespoon of mayonnaise	2 teaspoons of grainy mustard
1 tablespoon of butter	4 ciabatta buns

Cook mac & cheese as directed on the box. Combine the olives, raisins and green onions and pulse in a food processor until coarsely chopped, then add oil and vinegar; pulse a little more until incorporated. Refrigerate for ½ an hour. Spread each bun with mayonnaise and mustard. Layer the ham, cheese and a spoonful of mac & cheese. Melt butter in a large skillet on medium-low heat. Place sandwiches in to grill; pressing down slightly to flatten. Cook turning once until golden brown on both sides and the cheese is gooey – up to 15 minutes.

Enjoy!

Noodle Notes: ....

....

....

....

....

....

....

....

....

....

Grilled Jalapeño Mac & Cream Cheese

From thought to pot to plate: 40 minutes

Serves: 2

Ingredients:

your favorite box of mac & cheese	4 jalapeno peppers, seeded, cut lengthwise
1 tablespoon of butter	2 tablespoons of cream cheese
2 tablespoons of tortilla chips, crumbled	4 slices of sourdough bread

Cook mac & cheese as directed on the box. Set the oven on broil. Place the peppers on a sheet pan with the cut side facing down; broil until the outer layer of the skin blackens, about 8 minutes. Let cool and then remove the skins. Butter the outside of each slice of bread and spread the cream cheese on the inside; top with the jalapenos, a spoonful of mac & cheese, crumbled tortilla chips and the other slice of bread. Grill the sandwich on medium heat until both sides are golden brown, turning once.

Enjoy!

Noodle Notes: ....

....

....

....

....

....

....

....

....

....

....

....

5 Star Style
Mac & Cheese

We Be Jammin' Mac & Cheese

From thought to pot to plate: 40 minutes
Serves: 4

Ingredients:

your favorite box of mac & cheese	4 chicken breasts
2 cups of scallions, chopped	2 habanero chiles, diced
2 tablespoons of soy sauce	2 tablespoons of fresh lime juice
4 teaspoons of ground allspice	3 teaspoons of dry mustard
2 bay leaves	3 cloves of garlic, minced
2 teaspoons of dried thyme	1 teaspoon of cinnamon
1 teaspoon of cayenne pepper	1 teaspoon of black pepper
1 teaspoon of ground sage	1 teaspoon of nutmeg
1 tablespoon of sugar	¾ cup of white vinegar
½ cup of orange juice	vegetable oil for brushing the grill
1 can of black beans, rinsed and drained	

In a food processer, puree the scallion, chilies, soya sauce, vinegar, orange and lime juice and all the herbs and spices. Place the chicken in a large plastic bag and pour the marinade over it. Seal the bag, pressing out the excess air and let the chicken marinate for at least 24 hours, turning the bag several times throughout. Preheat an outdoor grill; making sure that the rack is oiled. Cook mac & cheese as directed on the box. Grill the chicken for 10 to 15 minutes a side and covered if possible. Baste the chicken with the leftover marinade. Serve jerk chicken on bed of mac & cheese with a side of black beans.

Ya mon!

Mike, Mac and Tenderloins a.k.a. "Date Night" Mac & Cheese

From thought to pot to plate: 35 minutes

Serves: 4

Ingredients:

your favorite box of mac & cheese	4 beef tenderloin steaks, cut 1" thick
2 tablespoons of butter	¼ cup of white onion, diced
¼ cup of beef broth	1 package of peppercorn sauce
1 teaspoon of dried marjoram, crushed	salt and pepper to taste
small bag of green salad	1 tbsp. of your favorite salad dressing

Cook mac & cheese as directed on the box. Trim the fat from the steaks. In a large skillet, melt butter over medium heat. Add the steaks and cook for 9 minutes of so, turning once (when juices pool on the top) and continuously basting in butter. This should give you medium-rare steaks. Once cooked to your liking, put the steaks on a platter to let the steaks rest and cover to keep warm. Leave the drippings in the skillet and follow the instructions on the package to make the peppercorn sauce. Stir the sauce, onions, marjoram and salt and pepper in the drippings, bringing it to a light boil, and reduce the heat to low for another 3 to 4 minutes. Serve sauce over steaks, with a side of mac & cheese.

Don't forget a salad! Serve in candlelight. This recipe is dedicated to my friend Mike, who had the Midas touch in the kitchen. Enjoy!

Surf and Turf Mac & Cheese Bake

From thought to pot to plate: 45 minutes

Serves: 4

Ingredients:

your favorite box of mac & cheese	2 beef sirloin steaks, sliced
1 cup of shrimp, peeled and deveined	1 can of green chiles, drained
½ cup of white onion, diced	2 cloves of garlic, minced
½ teaspoon of paprika	½ teaspoon of dry mustard
1 tablespoon of parsley, chopped	1 jalapeno, chopped
½ can of corn, drained	2 tablespoons of breadcrumbs
dash of olive oil	1 teaspoon of butter
salt and pepper to taste	½ cup of Parmesan cheese, grated

Preheat oven to 375°F. Cook mac & cheese as directed on the box. In a skillet, cook the steak in olive oil with the onion, jalapeno, corn and garlic. Add the paprika, mustard, parsley and mix together on low heat; then remove from heat. Next, sauté the shrimp in melted butter and diced green chiles. Combine all of the ingredients with the mac & cheese and top with breadcrumbs and Parmesan. Bake for about 15 minutes or until bubbling and the top is golden brown. Let stand for 10 minutes before serving.

Enjoy!

In-Laws Dinner Mac & Cheese

From thought to pot to plate: 40 minutes
Serves: 2

Ingredients:

your favorite box of mac & cheese	2 pork chops
salt and pepper to taste	1 teaspoon of rosemary, chopped
2 cloves of garlic, minced	½ lb. of fiddleheads*
½ cup of goat cheese, crumbled	dash of olive oil

Cook mac & cheese as directed on the box. In a large skillet on medium heat, cook the pork chops in a dash of olive oil with the rosemary, garlic, salt and pepper. Boil the fiddleheads in water for *at least* ten minutes, then drain. Combine the mac & cheese with the goat cheese and fiddleheads on a platter, with the seasoned pork chops on top.

* Fiddleheads are in season in the spring. They are available at the store. Do not pick your own, in case you pick the wrong type. That would be bad.

Enjoy!

Noodle Notes: ....
....
....
....
....
....
....
....
....
....
....
....

High Style Mac & Cheese

From thought to pot to plate: 35 minutes
Serves: 2

Ingredients:

your favorite box of mac & cheese	1½ cups of peeled and chopped
½ cup of pecans, chopped	½ cup of Gorgonzola, crumbled
½ cup of red onion, diced	2 teaspoons of thyme, chopped
2 teaspoons of honey	juice of one lemon
2 cups of fresh arugula	dash of olive oil
½ cup of breadcrumbs	salt and pepper to taste

Preheat oven to 350°F. Cook mac & cheese as directed on the box. Sauté the onion in olive oil; once soft, add the pecans, apples, thyme, honey, lemon juice, salt and pepper. Combine mixture with mac & cheese in a greased casserole dish, folding in the arugula and Gorgonzola. Top with breadcrumbs and bake for about 15 minutes or until bubbling and the top is golden brown. Let stand for 10 minutes before serving.

Enjoy!

Noodle Notes: ....

....

....

....

....

....

....

....

....

....

....

....

Herby Squash Mac & Cheese

From thought to pot to plate: 45 minutes

Serves: 2

Ingredients:

your favorite box of mac & cheese	2lbs. of butternut squash
½ cup of pine nuts	2 tablespoons of butter
1 tablespoon of rosemary, chopped	1 teaspoon of fresh ginger, grated
1 tablespoon of Dijon mustard	2 cups of Cheddar cheese, grated
salt and pepper to taste	

Preheat oven to 350°F. Cook mac & cheese as directed on the box. Once cooked, add the rosemary. Cut squash in half and scoop out the seeds. Place the squash cut-side down in a baking dish with about ¼ cup of water and bake until tender. In a separate bowl, roast the pine nuts until lightly browned – for about 2 minutes. Cut the squash into bite-sized pieces and combine with pine nuts, rosemary, mac & cheese, ginger, salt and pepper, along with 1½ cups of Cheddar. Place mixture in a casserole dish and top with the remaining ½ cup of Cheddar. Bake for about 15 minutes or until bubbling and the top is golden brown. Let stand for 10 minutes before serving.

Enjoy!

Noodle Notes: ....

....

....

....

....

....

....

....

....

Jersey Shore Mac & Cheese

From thought to pot to plate: 45 minutes
Serves: 2

Ingredients:

your favorite box of mac & cheese	1 cup of boardwalk fries
1 can of smoked oysters, drained	½ cup of canned clams, drained
1 cup of frozen calamari, breaded	1 wiener
frying oil	

Cook mac & cheese as directed on the box. Boil the wiener in a small pot; once cooked, slice and put in a skillet on medium heat, along with the clams and oysters and cook until the seafood is ready. In a separate, high-rimmed skillet place frozen breaded calamari in 1" of hot (but not smoking) oil and fry for about two minutes, turning frequently. Transfer to paper towel to drain. Combine the wieners, clam, oysters and fried calamari and serve on a bed of mac & cheese with a side of board-walk fries.

"Get some food. Feel better. Drink heavily." – J. Woww

Noodle Notes: ....

....

....

....

....

....

....

....

....

....

....

....

Mac & Cheese Deluxe Hawaiian Pizza

From thought to pot to plate: 40 minutes
Serves: 4

Ingredients:

your favorite box of mac & cheese	1 egg, beaten
1 cup of tomato sauce	¼ cup of sliced ham
1/3 cup of pineapple chunks	½ cup of red peppers, sliced
½ cup of fresh mushrooms, sliced	1 cup of mozzarella cheese, grated

Preheat oven to 350°F. Cook mac & cheese as directed on the box. Stir in the egg. Press the mac, egg and cheese mixture onto the bottom of a greased 12" pizza pan. Bake for 10 minutes. Remove from the oven and top the pasta shell with the remaining ingredients and cheese on top. Bake for about 15 minutes or until bubbling and the top is golden brown.

Hang ten people!

Maui Wowee Mac & Cheese

From thought to pot to plate: 30 minutes
Serves: 2

Ingredients:

your favorite box of mac & cheese	1 can of pineapple chunks, drained
2 cups of cooked ham, cubed	salt and pepper to taste
½ cup of red onion, diced	dash of hot sauce
dash of olive oil	½ cup of white Cheddar, grated

Preheat oven to 350°F. Cook mac & cheese as directed on the box. In a skillet sauté the onion in olive oil until soft. Combine the mac & cheese, onion, ham, pineapple, hot sauce, salt and pepper in a greased casserole dish. Top with Cheddar and bake for about 15 minutes or until bubbling and the top is golden brown. Let stand for 10 minutes before serving.

This is Emma's favorite!

Imperial Chicken Mac & Cheese

From thought to pot to plate: 50 minutes
Serves: 4

Ingredients:

your favorite box of mac & cheese	4 chicken breasts
1 small package of cream cheese	1 can of crab (picked over)
small bunch of spinach, chopped	2 green onions, sliced
salt and pepper to taste	dash of olive oil

Cook mac & cheese as directed on the box. Clean, stem and chop the spinach. Add olive oil to a heated skillet and cook spinach until wilted. Add crab, cream cheese and onions; season with salt and pepper and combine. Make a pocket in each chicken breast and stuff with an equal amount of filling. Bake in a 350 oven for 40 minutes until brown and cooked through. Serve with a side of mac and cheese.

Enjoy!

Noodle Notes: ....

....

....

....

....

....

....

....

....

....

....

....

....

....

Tartufo Blanco Mac & Cheese

From thought to pot to plate: 35 minutes
Serves: 2

Ingredients:

your favorite box of mac & cheese	1 teaspoon of butter
3 green onions, sliced	½ cup of white onion, diced
2 cloves of garlic, minced	½ cup of Fontina cheese, grated
1 teaspoon of white truffle oil	salt and pepper to taste
1 cup of panko breadcrumbs	½ cup of Gruyere cheese, grated

Preheat oven to 350°F. Cook mac & cheese as directed on the box. Sauté green onion, white onion and garlic in butter until tender. Combine with Fontina, salt and pepper and mac & cheese and put in a casserole dish and top with a combination of white truffle oil, panko breadcrumbs and Gruyere cheese. Bake for about 20 minutes or until bubbling and the top is golden brown. Let stand for 10 minutes before serving.

Enjoy!

Noodle Notes: ....

....

....

....

....

....

....

....

....

....

....

....

Fancy Filet Mignon with Mac & Cheese

From thought to pot to plate: 45 minutes
Serves: 4

Ingredients:

your favorite box of mac & cheese	4 (6-8oz.) filet mignon steaks
2 cloves of garlic, minced	½ cup of Worcestershire sauce
cracked black pepper to taste	1 tablespoon of Dijon mustard
4 to 6 slices of bacon, raw	

Preheat the BBQ. Cook mac & cheese as directed on the box. Marinate the steak in the garlic, Worcestershire sauce, pepper and mustard for about an hour in the refrigerator. Wrap the marinated filet mignons, with bacon; securing with a toothpick. Grill to your liking, turning once (when juices pool on the top side). Serve on a bed of mac & cheese.

Impress your friends! Impress your honey! Impress the whole neighbourhood!

Noodle Notes: ....

....

....

....

....

....

....

....

....

....

....

....

....

Renaissance Mac & Cheese

From thought to pot to plate: 35 minutes
Serves: 2

Ingredients:

box of mac & white Cheddar cheese	½ cup of pancetta, chopped
1 cup of smoked Gouda, grated	2 granny smith apples, chopped
1 teaspoon of rosemary, chopped	1 clove of garlic, minced
½ cup of white onion, diced	salt and pepper to taste

Preheat oven to 350°F. Cook mac & cheese as directed on the box. In a heated skillet, cook the pancetta until crispy and remove from pan; add onions and garlic and saute until tender. Combine the mac & cheese, ½ cup of Gouda, pancetta, chopped apples, rosemary, salt and pepper in a casserole dish and top with the remaining ½ cup of Gouda. Bake for about 15 minutes or until bubbling and the top is golden brown. Let stand for 10 minutes before serving.

Enjoy!

Noodle Notes: ....

....

....

....

....

....

....

....

....

....

....

Potato, Fennel and Bean Mac & Cheese

From thought to pot to plate: 45 minutes

Serves: 4

Ingredients:

your favorite box of mac & cheese	1lb. of fingerling potatoes, quartered
1 medium onion, chopped	1 small fennel bulb, chopped
dash of olive oil	2 cups of green beans, ½" pieces; blanched
3 celery stalks, chopped	1 English cucumber, peeled, chopped
½ cup of parsley, chopped	1 cup of plain Greek yogurt
1 teaspoon of paprika	juice of one lemon
salt and pepper to taste	

Preheat oven to 400°F. Place potatoes, onions and fennel on a sheet pan; drizzle with oil and toss to coat. Bake for 20-25 minutes until tender; stir occasionally. Cook mac & cheese as directed on the box. Put beans, celery, cucumbers, parsley and roasted vegetables in a large bowl. In small bowl, whisk together yogurt, paprika, lemon juice, salt and pepper. Pour over salad and toss to coat. Serve warm.

Enjoy!

Noodle Notes: ....

....

....

....

....

....

....

....

....

....

Artisan Mac & Cheese

From thought to pot to plate: 35 minutes

Serves: 2

Ingredients:

your favorite box of mac & cheese	½ cup of white onion, diced
dash of olive oil	1 teaspoon of rosemary, chopped
dash of nutmeg	1 tablespoon of grainy mustard
1 cup of Fontina cheese, grated	1 teaspoon of fresh rosemary, chopped
1 cup of breadcrumbs	½ cup of Parmesan cheese, grated
salt and pepper to taste	

Preheat oven to 350°F. Cook mac & cheese as directed on the box. In a heated skillet saute the onion, rosemary, salt, pepper and nutmeg in olive oil. Combine mixture with Fontina cheese and mac & cheese in a greased casserole dish. Cover the top with breadcrumbs and Parmesan cheese. Bake for about 25 minutes or until bubbling and the top is golden brown. Let stand for 10 minutes before serving.

Enjoy!

Noodle Notes: ....

....

....

....

....

....

....

....

....

....

....

Big Kahuna Mac & Cheese Tuna Bake

From thought to pot to plate: 35 minutes

Serves: 4

Ingredients:

your favorite box of mac & cheese	1 can of tuna, drained
1 can of cream of celery soup	½ cup of frozen peas, thawed
2 stalks of celery, chopped	salt and pepper to taste
suggested toppings	
crushed potato chips	fried chow mien noodles
crushed soda crackers	panko breadcrumbs

Preheat oven to 350°F. Cook mac & cheese as directed on the box. Add tuna, soup, peas, celery , salt and pepper to prepared mac and cheese; stir to combine. Put mixture into a casserole dish and add your favorite crunchy topping. Bake until bubbling and the top is golden.

Enjoy!

Noodle Notes: ....
....
....
....
....
....
....
....
....
....
....
....

Fortune 500 Mac & Cheese

From thought to pot to plate: 40 minutes
Serves: 6

Ingredients:

your favorite box of mac & cheese	dash of olive oil
2 cloves of garlic, minced	½ cup of celery, chopped
½ cup of fresh parsley, chopped	½ head of radicchio, shredded
1 tablespoon of water	½ cup walnuts, chopped
½ cup of Parmesan cheese, grated	½ cup of breadcrumbs
1 cup of cheese, crumbled	salt and pepper to taste

Preheat oven to 400°F. Cook mac & cheese as directed on the box. In a large skillet, sauté garlic, celery, parsley and radicchio in olive oil; add a tablespoon of water and cover on low heat until wilted – about 3 minutes. Remove from heat. Pulse walnuts, Parmesan and breadcrumbs in a food processor until crumbly. Combine with mac & cheese, salt, pepper and blue cheese. Put in a casserole dish and top with the Parmesan, walnuts and breadcrumbs. Bake for about 15 minutes or until bubbling and the top is golden brown. Let stand for 10 minutes before serving.

Enjoy!

Noodle Notes:

Mac & Cheese
Kickin' It Hostel Style

Mushroom Mac & Cheese Meatloaf

From thought to pot to plate: 60 minutes
Serves: 4

Ingredients:

your favorite box of mac & cheese	1lb. of lean ground beef
1 can of cream of mushroom soup	1 cup of fresh mushrooms, sliced
½ cup of white onion, diced	½ teaspoon of dried thyme
½ teaspoon of dried oregano	¼ cup of fresh parsley, chopped
dash of olive oil	1 clove garlic, minced
salt and pepper to taste	1 egg, beaten
1 tomato, sliced	½ cup of Parmesan cheese, grated

Preheat oven to 350°F. Cook mac & cheese as directed on the box. Blend in soup, thyme, oregano and parsley. Set aside. In a skillet brown the meat, add the onion, garlic and mushrooms and cook until soft. Stir in seasonings and remove from heat. Blend egg into slightly cooled meat mixture. In a 9" x 5" greased loaf pan, layer half of the macaroni in the pan and top with the meat mixture. Spread the remaining macaroni mixture over the meat and arrange the tomato slices on top. Sprinkle with Parmesan and bake for about 30 minutes or until bubbling and the top is golden brown. Let stand for 10 minutes before serving.

Magic mushroom mac meatloaf! Enjoy with a salad!

Champagne Tastes Beer Budget Mac & Cheese

From thought to pot to plate: 35 minutes

Serves: 2

Ingredients:

your favorite box of mac & cheese	¼ cup pancetta, chopped
dash of olive oil	salt and pepper to taste
1 teaspoon of thyme	½ cup of white onion, diced
2 cloves garlic, minced	¼ cup of champagne
1 cup of Gruyere cheese, grated	½ cup of Parmesan cheese, grated

Preheat oven to 350°F. Cook mac & cheese as directed on the box. In a medium saucepan, cook the pancetta for about 4 minutes or until crispy; set aside and put on a paper towel to drain. Add the onions and garlic to the pan and cook until soft. Combine mixture with the mac & cheese, along with the thyme, reserved pancetta, champagne and Gruyere. Put in a greased casserole dish and sprinkle the top with the Parmesan cheese. Bake for about 15 minutes or until bubbling and the top is golden brown. Let stand for 10 minutes before serving.

Congratulations! If you are reading this book you definitely have champagne tastes!

Yelpin' Helpin' Mac & Cheese

From thought to pot to plate: 25 minutes

Serves: 2

Ingredients:

your favorite box of mac & cheese	3 wieners
4 green onions, sliced	dash of hot sauce
20 goldfish crackers, crushed	½ cup of Cheddar cheese, grated

Preheat oven to 350°F. Cook mac & cheese as directed on the box. Boil wieners, slice into ½" thick pieces and mix into mac & cheese with green onions and hot sauce. Top with crushed goldfish crackers and the Cheddar cheese. Bake for about 15 minutes or until bubbling and the top is golden brown. Let stand for 5 minutes before serving.

Enjoy!

Pork, Beans and Burger Mac & Cheese

From thought to pot to plate: 25 minutes

Serves: 2

Ingredients:

your favorite box of mac & cheese	2 hamburger patties
can of pork 'n' beans	1 small bag of green salad
1 tbsp. of your favorite salad dressing	

Cook mac & cheese as directed on the box. In a separate pan heat can of pork 'n' beans on low, stirring occasionally. Add a tablespoon of oil to a skillet and fry patties until cooked. Divide mac & cheese between two plates, top with beef patties and cover with pork-n-beans. Serve with a dressed side salad.

Enjoy!

Mac & Cheese Hash Brown Casserole

From thought to pot to plate: 60 minutes
Serves: 4

Ingredients:

your favorite box of mac & cheese	1lb. of frozen hash browns, shredded
1 - 500ml carton of sour cream	2 cans of cream of mushroom soup
½ cup of butter, melted	1 cup of white onion, diced
2 cups of Cheddar cheese, grated	1 tablespoon of Parmesan cheese
salt and pepper to taste	

Preheat oven to 350°F. Cook mac & cheese as directed on the box. Mix the hash browns together with the mac & cheese, sour cream, mushroom soup, butter, onion and Cheddar cheese. Put the combination in a greased casserole dish. Sprinkle on the Parmesan cheese and bake for about 45 minutes or until browned on top and bubbling nicely.

Serve on the side with your main course – I recommend a salad or a defibrillator!

Noodle Notes: ....

....

....

....

....

....

....

....

....

....

....

....

Hangover Mac & Cheese

From thought to pot to plate: 35 minutes

Serves: 4

Ingredients:

your favorite box of mac & cheese	1 cup of mozzarella cheese, grated
1 cup of Cheddar cheese, grated	8 slices of bacon, chopped
stick of pepperoni, sliced	1 can of beer

Preheat oven to 350°F. Cook mac & cheese as directed on the box. Cook bacon in a skillet until crispy; set aside on paper towel to drain. Combine the mac & cheese, sliced pepperoni, ½ cup of the Cheddar, ½ cup of the mozzarella and bacon in a casserole dish. Cover with can of beer and the rest of the cheese. Bake for about 20 minutes or until bubbling and the top is golden brown. Let stand for 5 minutes before serving.

You'll want to eat this even when you don't have a hangover!

Mac & Cheese Pizza Pie

From thought to pot to plate: 45 minutes

Serves: 2

Ingredients:

your favorite box of mac & cheese	1 - 12" pizza shell
½ cup of pizza sauce	½ cup of Cheddar cheese, grated

Preheat oven to 350°F. Cook mac & cheese as directed on the box. Toast the pizza shell in the oven for about 5 minutes. Remove from oven, cover with pizza sauce, then top with mac & cheese, followed by the grated Cheddar. Bake until golden brown – approximately 10 minutes.

Enjoy!

Cheeseburger Mac & Cheese

From thought to pot to plate: 35 minutes
Serves: 2

Ingredients:

your favorite box of mac & cheese	1lb. of lean ground beef
2 tomatoes, sliced	1 cup of breadcrumbs
½ cup of white onion, diced	½ cup of Cheddar cheese, grated
dash of olive oil	salt and pepper to taste

Preheat oven to 350°F. Cook mac & cheese as directed on the box. Cook ground beef and onion in a heated skillet with olive oil. Spread the mac & cheese evenly on the bottom of the casserole dish. Layer on the meat mixture. Top with sliced tomatoes, breadcrumbs and cheese. Bake for about 15 minutes or until bubbling and the top is golden brown.

Why have just a cheeseburger when you can have a "mac & cheese" cheeseburger?

Noodle Notes:

Ham & Cauliflower Mac & Cheese

From thought to pot to plate: 35 minutes
Serves: 2

Ingredients:

your favorite box of mac & cheese	3 slices of cooked ham, cubed
2 cups of cauliflower, cut into florets	1 cup of frozen peas, thawed
½ cup of heavy cream	salt and pepper to taste
1 teaspoon of grainy mustard	½ cup of Swiss cheese, grated

Preheat oven to 350°F. Cook mac & cheese as directed on the box. Bring cauliflower to a boil and cook until tender; remove from pan. Combine the mac & cheese, cauliflower, ham, mustard, peas, salt, pepper and cream in a casserole dish. Sprinkle with cheese and bake for about 15 minutes or until bubbling and the top is golden brown. Let stand for 10 minutes before serving.

An instant classic! Enjoy!

Mac & Cheese Dog Skillet

From thought to pot to plate: 30 minutes
Serves: 2

Ingredients:

your favorite box of mac & cheese	4 wieners, sliced
½ cup of frozen peas, thawed	salt and pepper to taste
½ cup of white onion, diced	dash of olive oil

Cook mac & cheese as directed on the box. In heated skillet, sauté onion in oil, season with salt and pepper, along with the slice wieners. Once hot dogs are heated through, add the peas, stir together. Transfer the mac & cheese to a serving platter and top with sliced wiener mixture.

Mac-365 note: If you don't tell anyone you are making this… you'll get to eat the whole thing!

Bread Bowl Mac & Cheese

From thought to pot to plate: 20 minutes
Serves: 4

Ingredients:

your favorite box and mac & cheese	bread bowls, any type
salt and pepper to taste	

Cook mac & cheese as directed on the box. The hard part is deciding whether this is an appetizer or a main dish. Hollow out the bowl and fill with mac & cheese. Enjoy!

So delicious I even ate the dish it was served in!

Two Four Mac & Cheese

From thought to pot to plate: 40 minutes
Serves: 6

Ingredients:

4 boxes of your favorite mac & cheese	12 slices of bacon, chopped
2 cans of beer	2 cups of Cheddar cheese, grated
6 green onions, sliced	salt and pepper to taste

Preheat oven to 350°F. Cook mac & cheese as directed on the box. In a skillet, cook the bacon until crispy. Add green onions for the final minute. Put bacon and green onion mixture on a paper towel to drain. Combine the bacon, mac & cheese and 1½ cups of Cheddar in a large casserole dish. Pour beer evenly over the top and sprinkle the remaining cheese to finish. Bake for about 20 minutes or until bubbling and the top is golden brown. Let stand for 10 minutes before serving.

Enjoy!

Mac & Cheese Nip

From thought to pot to plate: 30 minutes

Serves: 2

Ingredients:

your favorite box of mac & cheese	1 tablespoon of butter
3 green onions, sliced	2 cloves of garlic, minced
1 cup of sour cream	2 tablespoons of Worcestershire sauce
1 cup of fresh parsley, chopped	salt and pepper to taste
½ cup of sharp Cheddar cheese, grated	

Cook mac & cheese as directed on the box. Melt butter in a skillet and sauté the green onion and garlic, until soft. Add the sour cream, Worcestershire, parsley, salt and pepper and stir until heated through. Pour mixture over a bed of mac & cheese and garnish with more parsley.

Enjoy!

Gone to the Dawgz Mac & Cheese

From thought to pot to plate: 35 minutes

Serves: 4

Ingredients:

your favorite box of mac & cheese	1 teaspoon of dry mustard
½ teaspoon of cayenne pepper	4 wieners
4 hot dog buns	½ cup of white onion, diced

Cook mac & cheese as directed on the box, adding the mustard and cayenne. Boil the wieners until cooked. Toast the buns. Serve mac & cheese as a condiment on the hot dog, along with diced onion, mustard, ketchup and relish – however you like your dawgz.

Dawg gone, is that good!

Mac & Cheese Baked Beans

From thought to pot to plate: 70 minutes
Serves: 4

Ingredients:

your favorite box of mac & cheese	1 cup of white onion, diced
4 slices bacon, chopped	½ cup fancy molasses
½ cup ketchup	¼ cup of grainy mustard
salt and pepper to taste	¼ teaspoon of red pepper flakes
1 can of navy beans, drained	1 can of red kidney beans, drained
dash of hot sauce	2 teaspoons of apple cider vinegar
1 tablespoon of brown sugar	1 bottle of Guinness
1 cup of BBQ sauce	

Preheat oven to 350°F. In a pan, cook bacon until crisp then place on paper towel to drain; in same pan, saute onion until soft. then sauté the onion until soft. Rinse and drain the beans. In a large, ovenproof ceramic bowl, combine the bacon, onion and the rest of the ingredients and cook on low for about an hour. Ten minutes before the beans are ready, cook mac & cheese as directed on the box. Serve beans on a bed of mac & cheese.

Enjoy!

If I Had a Million Dollars Mac & Cheese

From thought to pot to plate: 20 minutes

Serves: 2

Ingredients:

---

your favorite box of mac & cheese

2 slices of Canadian bacon, chopped

2 tablespoons of fancy Dijon ketchup

Cook mac & cheese as directed on the box. Cook bacon in a skillet until crispy; set aside on a paper towel to drain. Combine mac & cheese and bacon with the fanciest Dijon ketchup.

Enjoy!

Salt and Vinegar Mac & Cheese

From thought to pot to plate: 25 minutes

Serves: 2

Ingredients:

---

your favorite box of mac & cheese

1 box salt and vinegar chips, crumbled

½ cup of Cheddar cheese, grated

1 tablespoon of ketchup

1 dill pickle, sliced

Preheat oven to 350°F. Cook mac & cheese as directed on the box and transfer to a casserole dish, Top with the Cheddar and crumbled chips and bake for about 15 minutes or until the top is golden brown. Drizzle ketchup on top. Serve with sliced dill pickle. Seriously.

Enjoy!

Mac & Cheese BLT

From thought to pot to plate: 40 minutes

Serves: 2

Ingredients:

box of mac & white Cheddar cheese	½ cup of sun-dried tomatoes, chopped
5 slices bacon, chopped	salt and pepper to taste dash of hot sauce
½ cup of sour cream	½ cup of breadcrumbs
½ cup of Cheddar cheese, grated	2 cups of fresh spinach

Preheat oven to 375°F. Cook mac & cheese as directed on the box. Cook the bacon in a skillet until crispy and set aside on a paper towel to drain. Combine the bacon, sun dried tomatoes, spinach, hot sauce and sour cream with the mac & cheese in a greased casserole dish and top with grated Cheddar and breadcrumbs. Bake for about 20 minutes or until bubbling and the top is golden brown. Let stand for 10 minutes before serving.

Seriously good! Enjoy!

Noodle Notes:

Mac & Cheese Sweet Treats

You Bet Your Sweet Mac

From thought to pot to plate: 60 minutes
Serves: 4

Ingredients

2 boxes of your favorite mac & cheese	1 package of cream cheese
½ cup of vanilla yogurt	1 teaspoon of rum
1 teaspoon of vanilla extract	¾ cup of white chocolate
¼ cup sugar	1 apple, peeled, diced
½ cup of brown sugar	½ cup of shredded coconut
1/3 cup of flour	¼ teaspoon of salt
4 tbsp. of cold butter, in small pieces	½ cup of pecans, chopped

Preheat oven to 350°F. Cook mac as directed on the box (*reserve the cheese*) and set aside. In a medium sized bowl combine softened cream cheese, yogurt, rum, vanilla and sugar until smooth. Melt chocolate in microwave (for a few seconds) and stir into mixture, along with diced apple. Add macaroni, mix and place in a greased 9" x 13" inch pan. Make streusel topping by combining the brown sugar, coconut, flour, salt, butter and pecans to make the topping; working butter in the mixture with fingers until small clumps form. Add contents of the cheese package. Sprinkle topping over the mac mixture and bake for 20 minutes or until topping is lightly browned.

Enjoy!

Rocky Road Mac & Cheese

From thought to pot to plate: 25 minutes
Serves: 2

Ingredients:

your favorite box of mac & cheese	2 cups of marshmallows
1 cup of walnuts, crumbled	1 family size chocolate bar, crumbled

Preheat oven to 350°F. Cook the mac as directed on the box, without using the cheese pouch. Combine with other ingredients in a greased casserole dish. Bake for about 15 minutes or until the chocolate melts and the marshmallows are gooey.

Enjoy!

Pickles and Ice Cream Mac & Cheese

From thought to pot to plate: 25 minutes
Serves: 1

Ingredients:

your favorite box of mac & cheese	2 large dill pickles, sliced
dash of hot sauce	2 scoops of your favorite ice cream

Cook mac & cheese as directed on the box. Stir in chopped pickles and hot sauce. Serve with a side bowl of ice cream.

Enjoy!

Recipes Reference

Sometimes it's nice to make mac & cheese from scratch!

Mac & Cheese

From thought to pot to plate: 60 minutes
Ingredients:

1 cup of elbow macaroni	½ cup of butter
¼ cup of flour	2 cups of whole milk
salt and pepper to taste	1 teaspoon of dry mustard
½ cup of yellow onion, diced	½ teaspoon of paprika
1 cup of Cheddar cheese	1 egg, beaten
1 cup of panko breadcrumbs	1 tablespoon of fresh parsley, chopped

Preheat oven to 375°F. Cook macaroni as directed on the package to *al dente* consistency; drain. Melt butter in a saucepan and whisk in the flour and mustard until smooth. Gradually whisk in the milk and onion and cook until thick and smooth; season with salt, pepper and paprika and add egg. Stir in ¾ of the cheese and combine with cooked macaroni. Transfer mixture to a greased casserole dish and top with the remaining cheese, panko breadcrumbs and parsley. Bake for 25 minutes or until heated through and golden brown. Let stand for 10 minutes before serving.

Pesto

Ingredients:

1 cup of fresh basil leaves, packed	2 cloves of garlic, minced
½ cup of virgin olive oil	½ cup of toasted pine nuts
¼ cup of Parmesan cheese, grated	¼ cup of white wine

Combine the ingredients and pulse in a food processor.

Tzatziki

Ingredients:

---

3 cucumbers, peeled, cored and grated

½ cup of red onion, diced

1 tablespoon of fresh dill, chopped

salt and pepper to taste

3 cloves of garlic, minced

½ cup of Greek yogurt

1 teaspoon of lemon juice

Combine the grated cucumber, garlic, onion, yogurt, dill, lemon, lemon juice, salt and pepper and serve cold.

Noodle Notes: ....

....

....

....

....

....

....

....

....

....

....

....

....

....

....

....

....

....

Uses for Cheese Powder*

- Add to a quiche recipe

- Add to breadcrumbs to season

- Add to cornmeal for bread or muffins

- Add to cream cheese to make a cheese ball

- Add to cream soups (i.e. broccoli, celery, mushroom)

- Add to mashed potatoes

- Add to your favorite bread machine recipe for cheese bread

- Coat chicken or tofu

- Make savory muffins

- Mix with chili powder, cayenne pepper and or dried mustard to sprinkle over popcorn

- Prepare as sauce for steamed cauliflower or broccoli

- Sprinkle into pasta salad

- Sprinkle on stuffed mushroom caps

- Stir into a white sauce (i.e. for pasta)

- Topping for baked potatoes or French fries

- Whisk into eggs before scrambling or making an omelet

* Powdered cheese is 1/3 stronger than cheese (i.e. if recipe calls for 12oz. of cheese, use 8oz. of powder).

Closing Remarks from Mr. Mac

Well, you have come to the end of a marathon of noodle cooking and eating and just having fun! Around the world in a bowl! My travels inspired me to first start writing about my life, so I could share with my future grandchildren… if I ever have any. As I was writing, mac kept popping up in my thoughts, going through customs with suitcases full of mac & cheese – making me laugh at myself and the reaction of the customs agents! I didn't change the direction of my writing, I just decided to write recipes related to my travels. Anyone who knows me will know why I did it this way, every recipe has its own story between the lines. One day I will fill in the blanks and write a book on the places I've been and seen, then you will be able to thumb through Mac-365 and match the recipe to where I was in the world. Kind of like a "Where's Waldo?" of mac & cheese.

Thank you for reading my stories and trying out my recipes – I'm sure your family – wife, husband, girlfriend, father, aunts, uncles, second cousin twice removed – will love them.

Please visit our website at www.macme365.com to have your say, enter contests and see our blog. Join Mr. Mac at his Twitter feed @macme365.

Yours, Kenneth (Mac) Cardell